THE ROAD TO PUBLICATION
A Writer's Navigation Guide

CLAIRE GEM

Erato Publishing
All rights reserved

THE ROAD TO PUBLICATION: A Writer's Navigation Guide
Copyright ©2017
CLAIRE GEM
Copyright ©2017 Frances Brown

Exclusive Cover Design ©2017 Frances S. Brown
Edited by: Allie Rottman, Silver Sparrow Editorial

Although the author and publisher have made every effort to ensure that the information in this book was correct at press time, the author and publisher do not assume and hereby disclaim any liability to any party for any loss, damage, or disruption caused by errors or omissions, whether such errors or omissions result from negligence, accident, or any other cause.

All rights reserved. No part of this publication may be reproduced, stored in a retrieval system, or transmitted in any form or by any means (electronic, mechanical, photocopying, recording, or otherwise) without the prior written permission of both the copyright owner and the publisher. The only exception is brief quotations in printed reviews.
The scanning, uploading, and distribution of this book via the Internet or via any other means without the permission of the publisher is illegal and punishable by law. Please purchase only authorized electronic editions, and do not participate in or encourage electronic piracy of copyrighted materials.
ISBN: 978-0-9974326-5-7

The publisher does not have any control over and does not assume any responsibility for author or third-party websites or their content.

Dedication

I am officially releasing this book on the date of my father's death, Frank Del Negro, Sr. who died on March 17th of 2001. This may sound macabre, but if anyone would appreciate being honored on this date (other than Saint Patrick), it would be my dad. He was my inspiration, my biggest hero, and the whole reason I ever had the guts to do anything in my entire life. He also gifted me with the perseverance to succeed—particularly to sit down and write a book—and then to publish it.

Frank Del Negro, Sr. was a brilliant, highly educated man with a vocabulary like no one I've ever met in my life. It is for him that I write this book. It is in his memory that I will, every single day of my life, continue to pen my thoughts, dreams, and crazy imaginings, because if he taught me nothing else, my father taught me to be a dreamer.

Thank you, Daddy. You may be gone from this earth, but you will always live on in my heart.

Contents

The Road to Publication: Part I

Introduction

A Brief History of the Publishing Industry

The Question—First Ask Yourself: Why?

Write the Best Book You Can Write

Your Choices: Traditional Publishing, Route A

Your Choices: Traditional Publishing, Route B

Your Choices: Subsidy or Vanity Publishing, and Assisted Self-Publishing

Your Choices: Do It Yourself—The Ugly, Bastard StepChild

Darlings and Puppies

The Perfect Editor

Between the Covers

The Road to Publication: Part II—A Guide for the Self-Published Author

Quality Control—After the Editor

Formatting: Digital

Formatting: Print

Get on Your Soapbox, or Your Books Needs Wings Before It Can Fly

Get Ready for The Perfect Takeoff

Gaining Credibility: Reviews and Contests

Closing Thoughts

A Note from the Author & References

Claire Gem

The Road to Publication: Part I
A Writer's Navigation Guide

Writing is an art, and should be taught as such.

These words comprise the first sentence of my Statement of Philosophy in regards to the craft of creative writing. Over the last ten years, in my struggle to achieve the status of "published author," it has become painfully obvious to me that I'd embarked on the journey clutching the wrong, stinking road map in my shaking, sweaty hands.

My daytime career, for the past 36 years, has been in the field of laboratory science. And although my zodiac sign is *not* Gemini, I do, admittedly, suffer from a split personality. No matter how fascinating, challenging, and fulfilling I have found my work in scientific research is, there has always been another side to me—the creative side. About ten years ago, having reached a pinnacle in my scientific career, I realized I was still unfulfilled.

The stories inside my head just wouldn't wait any longer to be told.

Naturally, my first instinct when learning a new skill—this writing thing—was to approach the task scientifically. There has to be a protocol, right? A recipe? A simple formula that would allow me to go from "wannabe fiction writer" to "multi-published, award-winning author"? Is there? No. And I learned that very, tough lesson the hard way.

The Road to Publication

And unfortunately, at least at the beginning, there weren't too many authors who had already achieved their lofty goals who would take the time or the trouble to clue me in as to which route was the best.

It was like this big, deep, dark secret path into a world of mystical wonder:

~ P~U~B~L~I~C~A~T~I~O~N~!

Only duly vetted and accepted members were allowed accessed to the map. The rest of us were left standing on the side of the Road to Publication with brows furrowed, thumbs out.

So many times along the way, when I found myself bumping into dead-ends and trapped in blind alleys, I thought, "Surely, there must be someone out there willing to put this whole crazy, elusive journey—the road to publication—into a logical perspective." I took courses, went to seminars, read many books written by other authors, and all that did help enlighten me. The process, however, was less like a light bulb suddenly popping on, and more like someone handing me a mini-flashlight—one with half-dead batteries—and waving it vaguely toward a long, dark tunnel.

The goal of this book is not to teach you how to write—if you've come to these pages, you are already a Word Artist. I hope to inspire you, and offer guidance on whatever journey you'd like to take with your writing. My wish is to encourage every person who has ever dreamed of seeing his or her creative writing in print to surge forward, fear and uncertainty be damned.

I will share some of my experiences, but this is not a memoir. Nor is it a flagrant touting of my accomplishments in the world of publication—in truth, I've only just begun to scratch the surface of my aspirations as a writer. I tried to write *the book I wish I could have found* way back at the beginning of my own writing journey. My hope is that my words will enlighten, guide, and reassure you on your own personal path through this treacherous, mysterious expedition called The Road to Publication.

A Brief History of the Publishing Industry

In order to provide you, the aspiring fiction author, with a roadmap—one with which to navigate through the treacherous forest of publishing, I feel you need an overview. You need to understand the lay of the land, to coin a phrase (or use a cliché). Only then will you be able to make smart decisions as to which route you want to take in order to reach your pot of gold, i.e., your published book.

Basically, here's how it goes:

Early 19th Century: Not only did you need to have the ability to write, the perseverance to finish a manuscript, and the courage to find a publisher willing to publish your work—you also had to be male. Example: Charlotte Brontë published her works under the name Currer Bell. A publisher would never have considered printing a book by a "Charlotte." Thank goodness we've come a long way since then.

Late 19th into the 20th Century: The term "publisher" became synonymous with the "Big Six" – Hachette Book Group, Harper Collins, Macmillan, Penguin, Random House, and Simon & Schuster. If you wrote a book and wanted it published, you sent queries to the editors of one of these Big Six, and you waited. And prayed. And waited some more.

Mid-20th and into the Early 21st Centuries: The **Vanity or Subsidy Press** came into being. These are small, independent (as in, independent of the Big Six) publishing houses (more like small businesses). These companies will publish anyone who has the money to pay for their services: editing, formatting, cover production, and printing. It will cost the author anywhere from hundreds to many thousands of dollars for these services. The majority of subsidy presses deal primarily with physical, printed books.

In reality, this method is self-publishing, because most of these companies will publish anyone who can pay for their services. The process basically consists of sub-contracting the procedure of publishing—everything that happens between writing The End through the production of a printed book—out to presumably experienced professionals.

In the end, it's a self-published book. The only difference is who pressed the "publish" button.

Early 21st Century: The Big Six shrank to the Big Five when Penguin and Random House merged in 2013. And by then, acquiring an **Agent** had become an increasingly necessary step in the process. No longer could you query the Big Five publishers directly. First you needed to locate an agent who specialized in your type of book, and send query letters to *them*. Then you waited. And prayed. Once you secured an agent, it was *the agent* who pitched your book to the Big Five editors. And then, you waited and prayed some more.

21st Century: Like mushrooms, the world is now sprouting dozens, if not hundreds, of **Independent Presses**. Started by smart, small business owners who saw a niche in the market of publishing, they have filled the space quite nicely. An Independent Press is the "halfway house" between the Big Five and a Subsidy Press.

Make no mistake: they will not publish just anybody. Independent presses each have their own standards by which they evaluate submissions from prospective authors. But these "standards" are much less difficult to attain than those of the Big Five.

This is not to say an independent publisher's standards are lower, by any means. It's just that they are different. Independent Presses have less to lose, i.e., are gambling with lower stakes, than the Big Five publisher. These small presses usually specialize in a particular genre. They offer no advances. They do provide, however, all the services needed to get the book published at no cost to the author. I repeat: **at no cost up front to the author**. If you find yourself dealing with publisher who is asking for a check, this is a subsidy publisher.

2007: Amazon launched the Kindle eReader, along with its self-publishing platform, Kindle Direct Publishing. The era of self-publishing was born.

And the world of publishing got turned on its ear.

What effect has this had on the hierarchy created by the Big Five? At first, the publishing industry claimed that there was no effect. Kindle and self-publishing was a fad that would burn itself out, and the world of publishing would return to business as usual.

It hasn't.

Between 2008 and 2010, the *New York Times* reported that eBook sales had skyrocketed, up 1260%. During that time, Barnes & Noble's eReader, the Nook, debuted, as well as Apple's iPad—all devices designed for eBook consumption. A shift occurred in the world of publishing, causing a crack in the traditional paradigm with the ominous potential of the San Andreas Fault.

For a short time, the world held their breath, wondering if the paper book would go the way of the dinosaurs. Independent bookstores all over the world closed their doors, and sales for the major chains dropped. In 2011, Waldenbooks, a Borders Books subsidiary, went bankrupt. And even today, although Barnes & Noble remains the largest retail bookseller in the United States, their profile has adjusted considerably to the times.

B&N now sells not only paper books, eBooks, and magazines, but toys, games, music, movies, and all sorts of stationary products geared toward the reader/writer. With the addition of Starbucks cafes and free Wi-Fi, B&N is no longer just a bookstore, but a gathering place for readers and writers—which is why they continue to survive, even thrive in the changing landscape.

Will paper books ever disappear entirely? Extremely doubtful. But as the masses age, the convenience, affordability, and versatility of the digital book will continue to grow in popularity. EBooks are eco-friendly—not a single tree's life is lost in their production. They don't take up any space on your bookshelves. There are no constraints on your book shopping or buying habits. One can decide, at two a.m. on a holiday, on a book they want to read—and *buy it, instantly*. No shipping fees, no waiting time. And instead of toting a heavy backpack filled with paper books along, one can store as many digital books on their chosen reading device as they want. Even their phone. (Well, that does depend on digital storage space, but still . . .)

Paper books may not be on the road to extinction, but the eBook is definitely not going anywhere.

What does this mean to the aspiring author? We now have choices—lots of them—when deciding on a path to publication. Which route do you want to take?

First, just as in crafting a quality piece of fiction, you must decide the main character's goals and motivation. The main character is you. Let's explore the reasons why you might want to pursue the road to publication.

The Question—First Ask Yourself: WHY?

Why do you want to write? I mean, beyond the age-old practice of journaling or diary entries. Do you have a story you want to tell? *Need* to tell? Then you first must decide which of the following describes your goal. Which one describes you best?

A Creative Writer: One who wishes to express their imagination through the art of writing, through the medium of words. A visual artist uses pencil or paint or clay. The musician creates with musical notes. A Creative Writer is a Word Artist, one who achieves fulfillment by the simple act of **creating their art**, even if only as a hobby.

An Author: An Author is a Word Artist who's willing to take their show on the road—a Creative Writer who possesses the burning desire to promote their work, the courage to risk ridicule and criticism, and the determination and tenacity to pursue their own personal goal, ruthlessly, in regards to their art.

Their own personal goal. Yes, each author has their own shiny pot of gold at the end of the publication rainbow. It could be as simple as seeing their Word Art in print, between glossy covers with their name on the front. A treasure, a keepsake they can share with friends or family. One they can display proudly in their living room. Pass down to their grandchildren.

Some authors' goals are more complicated—many dream of seeing stacks of those shiny books piled high on the front display tables at their local bookstore—surrounded, of course, by anxious fans. Others yearn for the prestige associated with winning a contest, or hitting a bestseller list.

Then there those who some might consider mercenaries: these writers want to make money with their Word Art. Now, I don't have to tell you how elusive that goal is to attain. Just ask the ghost of poor Vincent Van Gogh, who only sold one painting during his lifetime for the equivalent of about eighty American dollars. He died pitiful and penniless. It only took the world about fifty years or so to discover what they'd lost in an artistic genius like Van Gogh.

Still, it is possible to make money with words, along many different avenues. Freelance writers get paid to write articles for magazines. Some bloggers become so popular they find sponsors to pay them for advertising space on their blogs—and have retired on the passive income from these "virtual billboards." There are dozens, probably hundreds of contests out there with hefty cash prizes—if you win. After you pay their entry fees.

I dabbled in all of these ways to make money with my writing, and was moderately successful in several. But bottom line was this: it wasn't what I wanted to do. I wanted to write novels—fiction. I wanted to create imaginary worlds and people and situations. I wanted to evoke emotion in my readers, leaving them smiling through happy tears when they reached The End.

And I wanted to make enough money selling these books to be a full-time author. To live the author's life: write, travel, host book signings, and meet people who love my books.

Is this an unreasonable goal? Perhaps—I'm still on the journey. But I do live an author's life, more and more daily. And I'm loving every day spent on the road.

What I have learned so far is that unlike what many will tell you, it's not an impossible dream. You do not need to be John Grisham or Stephen King or Jodi Picoult or J.K. Rowling to live the life of an author. Perhaps ten years ago this was the case. But not today. The rules of the game have changed.

There are more options than ever before for an aspiring author to attain their goals.

Which brings us to a more difficult question: *what* is it that you want to write? Or have already written? Do you know what genre your manuscript falls into? Is it literary, or is it genre/mainstream?

What's the difference, anyway?

This is an age-old argument that, if you bring it up at a cocktail party, has the potential to stir up as much turbulence as a strongly biased, political statement. In a segment of the Writer's Toolbox (Gotham's Writers Workshop), the difference is explained thus:

"A genre is a category of literature, such as mystery, suspense, science fiction or horror. Each genre has its own conventions. Romance, for example, focuses on romantic love between two people and often ends positively. Generally, **genre fiction tends to place value on entertainment** and, as a result, it tends to be more popular with mass audiences.

Literary fiction, on the other hand, is a bit trickier to define. In general, it **emphasizes meaning over entertainment**. Literary fiction also aspires toward art. Of course, that abstract of "art" is where things get most tricky. What is art? In fiction, it can be defined as interesting and deep manifestations of the elements of craft: dimensional characters, a pleasing arc of tension, evocative language and thematic purpose.

Of course, literary and genre fiction aren't exclusive of one another. A work of genre fiction can be literary as well. Jane Austin, for example, wrote literary romances, such as *Pride and Prejudice*."

Other sources claim:

- Literary fiction is largely character-driven, while genre fiction is plot-driven.

- Literary works rely more heavily on setting descriptions and eloquent prose.

- The pacing of literary fiction tends to be slower (another source was a little more blunt: "Nothing much happens.")

Genre, or Mainstream Fiction, in comparison, is described as:

- Appealing to a wider audience, i.e., the general public. For this reason, some fans of literary fiction consider it less worthy of merit.

- Faster paced, with more emphasis on action than description.

- Divided into specific sub-genres—romance, mystery, horror, science fiction, westerns—thus appealing to fans of these genres because these readers know what kind of story they are getting.

So now that I've gotten you totally confused about what the heck it is that you want to write, I will ask you another question—one that might be easier to answer, and may give you the answer to the first question: what do you like to *read*?

Chances are, whatever kind of books you love, have read more than once, and consider keepers on your bookshelf are the kinds of book you would probably be best at writing. Passion, in any author's work, is what makes the stories vibrant. No matter what you write, make that book the best it can possibly be.

How do you do that? Read on . . .

Claire Gem

Write the Best Book You Can Write

This subject could, and will, fill an entire book of its own (coming soon—sign up for my mailing list so you'll be the first to know when it's available). I spent thirty months, and tens of thousands of dollars, to learn how to do just that—and to achieve those three little letters behind my name: MFA. Master of Fine Arts in Creative Writing.

Was it worth it? Definitely. Is it a must-have prerequisite to writing a great book? No.

Have I done that yet? Dunno. Ask my readers.

There are plenty of writing craft books and seminars on the subject where you can obtain the specific knowledge you will need to excel in writing whatever kind of book you want to write. There are writing groups and critique groups. Countless courses are available, both online and locally.

But I will share with you here three nuggets of wisdom I have gleaned from those months in graduate school, and in the school of hard knocks in the years since then. Do these things, and you're on your way to developing an authorial mindset.

1. **READ**. And read, and read, and read. Whatever kind of book you want to write, find
other books in the same genre, and read them. There is no better way to learn how to write a great book than to read great books. And you will discover—all of them aren't great. At least, not in your personal opinion as a reader.

But after about the fifteenth or twentieth one, you will start to recognize which authors' styles, and voices, you like. Which ones grab you and keep you up until three a.m. when your alarm clock will go off in two hours . . .and which ones put you to sleep more effectively than a cup of chamomile tea (or decaffeinated Chai).

2. **LISTEN**. Yes, I'm talking about audiobooks. I am a firm believer that reading a book with one's eyes is radically different from consuming those words with one's ears. *Even the same, exact book.*

Amazon has a wonderful program now called Whispersync that allows you to purchase an audiobook and a digital version of the print book, together, for a reduced price. Then your Kindle device syncs with the Audible app, allowing you to switch back and forth between reading and listening without losing your place. Ain't technology amazing?

3. **WATCH**. Read a favorite book that's now a movie? Go see it, or rent it. Seen a great movie that's also available in book format? Read it. Analyze the difference between how the author told the story with words, and how the director, actors and actresses portrayed the tale on the screen. The text vs. the cinematography are almost never exactly the same.

Which one did you like better? And more importantly, why?

I consider these the three, magic ways to improve the quality of your writing: Read, Listen, and Watch.

The idea here is not to copy another writer's work—that's called plagiarism. But if you find a particular style you love, your own writing will naturally model itself in that direction. What will emerge is your own, unique authorial voice, and one you already know you love. If you love what you are writing, that passion, that enthusiasm, will bleed onto the page. And your reader will feel it too.

Remember: Each and every individual reader has their own likes and dislikes. That's what guarantees every, single author the chance of appealing to at least one subset of the reading public. For every unique, authorial voice, there is a unique, passionate fan.

The Rules

If you, like me, harbor a few mercenary tendencies, you'll want to sell these books that you spent so many hours toiling over. Writing the best book you can write will then also involve some research on your part—some *market* research. At the very least, you want your book to match the basic format of other books in your chosen genre.

At a recent multi-author event, I met a young woman who had written and published a paranormal, young adult novel. Her cover was stunning, and the marketing setup of her table was equally as remarkable. A veritable Halloween haunted house attraction, the display was complete with a bowl of fake blood and glowing skull. And it did draw a lot of attention.

But unfortunately, I don't think she sold many books that day. I'm not sure how many she *will* sell, because of a single and critically limiting factor: the book was about three inches thick, comprising the better part of one thousand pages. And it was not a large-print format.

I personally don't know of any reader, particularly one in this author's target age group, who would make it through a 1000-page book.

Sure, there have been exceptions. J.R.R. Tolkien's *Lord of the Rings* is over 1200 pages long. Marcel Proust's *In Search of Lost Time* weighs in at 3092 pages. And L. Ron Hubbard's *Mission Earth* stretches to nearly 4000 pages—but all of these novels were written and published, initially, in series format, i.e., smaller chunks at a time.

I find it difficult to believe a reader, particularly a young reader, would commit to a 1000-page novel by an unknown author. A book this length translates to approximately 250,000 words.

The average word count for a YA novel is between 55-90K words, or 220-360 pages. It's the length expected by the reading audience. There is a similar "average length" for every genre out there. This particular young author, whose imagination, no doubt, is fertile for writing stories of epic proportion, would have been much wiser to split her three-inch-thick tome into three or four shorter episodes.

Here are the average, expected word counts for a few common fiction genres. Bear in mind that word count divided by 250 words per page will approximate the page count.

Children's picture books:	< 1000 words
Middle Grade:	25-40K
Young Adult fiction:	55-90K
New Adult:	60-85K

Novella:	20-50K, generally <40K
Romance:	40-100K, though 70-100K is considered mainstream
Paranormal:	75-95K
Horror:	80-100K
Literary/Women's Fiction:	80-110K
Science Fiction & Fantasy:	90-120K
Crime Fiction:	90-100K
Historical:	100-150K

These numbers are, of course, guidelines—not only generated by the publishing industry, but also by the expectations of the readers of those genres. When a prospective buyer picks up a paranormal YA book by an unknown, debut author, and it weighs more than their backpack full of textbooks, it's doubtful they will be up for the challenge. Plus, a book of this size costs a lot to print, and no doubt a cover price over $30 would discourage all but the most affluent reader.

For all these reasons, the young lady at the author event may have difficulty establishing a fan base.

This raises another question on the subject of writing guidelines. There is some controversy as to which comes first—the book or the audience? Should an author endeavor to write what their intended audience expects? To a degree, yes.

A successful author will have studied his or her chosen genre—by READING, LISTENING, and WATCHING—until they have a pretty good idea of what that audience wants and expects. Women's fiction subscribers want the emotionally poignant telling of a woman's personal journey. Science fiction readers expect an otherworldly or futuristic adventure. And fans of historical fiction want an epic story to take place in a bygone era, preferably one sufficiently researched to be historically accurate.

History, by the way, is a wonderful place to find story seeds, and not just for historical novels. My book, *Mining History: A Story Seed*

Goldmine, is coming soon—sign up for my newsletter so you're the first to know when it becomes available.

But how about approaching this concept from the other direction? Instead of writing toward your audience, how about taking a shortcut? It's easy enough to scan the *New York Times* Best Sellers Lists to see which books are hot, as well as consistent, sellers. Why not just write a book like one of those? *So what* if you're not really passionate about legal thrillers? It's making John Grisham a ton of money. Surely, writing one of those is the way to quick, easy stardom.

Don't do this.

For one thing, unless you're an attorney, like Grisham, you can't assume you'd be *even a little* qualified to write this sort of novel. And more importantly, Attorney Grisham is not only highly educated in his field, but he is also passionate about writing legal thrillers.

Sure, if you really do love legal thrillers, and have READ, LISTENED to, and WATCHED **about a hundred or so of them**, you could try your hand at writing one. And you might well be very successful. But don't choose a runaway bestseller and try to emulate it. Not unless you, as a writer, are truly passionate about writing those kinds of stories.

Remember, it's the writer's passion bleeding onto the page that touches the hearts of readers. If the writer didn't pour emotion into the book, the consumer certainly won't experience any in the reading. And the bottom line is this: readers of fiction want an emotional journey. If they don't get one, they won't pick up another book with your name on the cover. They probably won't even finish the first one.

The Road to Publication

Recap
1. Decide what genre you love. That's the one you should write.
2. READ, LISTEN to, & WATCH as many titles in your genre as you can get your eyes and ears on.
3. Study the guidelines for your chosen genre, starting with length. Endeavor to shape your story into a package that the consumer of this kind of book wants, and expects. Become educated, and remain aware of "The Rules" pertaining to your chosen genre.

BUT:

Don't worry about word counts, sentence structure, grammar, or all the other semantics on that first draft. **Write with abandon**. Pour your heart into the first telling, without agonizing over making it perfect.

Here is where you capture the essence of your true Word Art. Your writing style. Your voice. Let it flow, writing as though no one else will ever see it.

The "making it perfect" part cannot begin until you've written THE END. Only then, when you have a framework, should you begin your process of revision. Editing. Shaping and molding. It's hard work, and it can be painful.

Do you have that first draft finished? Have you written an author's very favorite two words in the whole world—THE END? Good.

Now it's time to start hacking through the weeds growing over your path to publication. But before we grab the scythe, we first have to establish which road you're going to take. It will definitely determine the size and shape of your tool.

Your Choices—Traditional Publishing: Route A

This is by far the most popular way a writer wants to be published. It's the real deal and, although probably the most difficult to achieve, is unbeatable as far as "legitimizing" you as an author. To most, it epitomizes the authorial "pot of gold."

How does one embark on this quest?

As mentioned, gone are the days when a writer could query a Big Five publisher directly. At least, for the most part. Nowadays, the only way to get your book under the nose of a New York publisher is through two avenues:

1. Query—and secure—a literary agent.
2. Pitch directly to an agent and/or editor who attends a writer's conference. *And secure their representation.*

Let's take them in order.

Hiring an Agent – the Query Letter

This process is more complicated, and more time-consuming, than one might assume. For unlike hiring a chauffeur, it's not as simple as scrolling through the phone listings, choosing a few companies, test driving them, and then choosing the best fit.

With literary agents, it's more like *they* have to accept *you* as a client.

Literary agents have specialties. Favorite genres of books they like to represent. So, the first step is to identify a list of agents who:

a. Represent your book's genre, and
b. Are accepting new clients

How does one access this information? The classic and most respected source is The Writer's Market, which is available as a huge, heavy tome at your local bookstore. You can also order it online. Or, you can subscribe for monthly access to the most current information at www.writersmarket.com.

The book, and the website, are well-organized and comprehensive. The website is searchable by several different parameters, including genre. You can also determine (online) if the particular agent is, right now, *today*, taking new clients. This information changes from month to month, and will not always be accurate in the print version.

In the beginning, when I had first completed a novel and was ready to "shop it around" (or thought I was), I went to the library and used their copy of The Writer's Market. Later on, I paid the monthly membership fee (which is minimal) to access the information. I made a list of agents—usually six at a time—and set about the process of writing and sending out Query Letters.

There are numerous websites and books dedicated to the writing of the Query Letter. I will not go into the specifics here, mostly because the format and contents vary according to your book's genre. My suggestion is to do online searches for "Query Letter + (your genre)" and see what you come up with. Follow the guidelines, and, well...you're a writer. Craft a knock-their-socks off query letter and either mail or email the query (the agent's guidelines will specify which they prefer).

Keep in mind the term "simultaneous submissions." Some agents will specify they do not accept queries that are also being sent to other agents at the same time. This can slow down your progress considerably, because...

You should not expect immediate replies. In reality, don't stake your grandmother's jewelry on receiving any replies at all. Of the 100+ query letters I sent to various agents over the years, I received approximately a dozen actual responses. Eight were rejections—*form letter* rejections. Talk about ruining your day...

Three replies were requests for a "partial." This, in my case, consisted of anywhere from the first three chapters to the first 75 pages. After I did a happy dance and ran through the house screaming, clutching the letter in my sweaty hand, I honed and polished and sweated over that "partial" for two weeks before sending it off. Two of the agents replied—some weeks or months later—with rejection letters. At least this time, the letters were personally written.

One even included some suggestions as to how I might improve my work. The third agent never granted me the courtesy of a "thanks, but no thanks."

At least, not yet. But I haven't given up hope—that was only a few years ago.

Bear in mind that this entire process, from the sending of the query letter, to receiving a reply, of any kind, took anywhere from two weeks to over a year. One of the rejection emails I received was fourteen months after query. I'd even forgotten that I'd queried the agent in the first place—and for what book!

Ironically, I'd already secured a contract on that book by then anyway. So, no Agent X, I will not be submitting a partial for your perusal. I've already signed with someone else.

Pitching at a Conference

This is the second route one can pursue in their quest to secure a contract with a major, traditional publisher. I've done it about a half dozen times, at three different conferences.

I can tell you this: it's not for the faint of heart.

Each conference invites numerous editors and agents who specialize in whatever genre the conference represents. Registrants are placed on a first-come, first-serve list (preference usually given to members in good standing of the hosting organization). The aspiring author vies for one or two "spots," i.e., appointments to pitch, face-to-face, to the editor or agent of their choice. These pitching appointments range from 8-12 minutes in length. And yes, they do time them. Down to the seconds.

That's it. You have only a very few, precious moments in which to smile and introduce yourself to the agent or editor, grab their attention, and describe your 75-120K word novel succinctly enough to pique their interest. Breathing is optional.

The very first time I pitched was at the New England Romance Writer's Conference a number of years ago. I paid my registration fee, hotel room, and other related travel expenses, and took my Word Art on the road. Being a new member, I secured only one spot, but a good one: with an editor from Harlequin.

I've never been more nervous in my entire life.

The folks who hear pitches at conferences, though, are seasoned and very sympathetic professionals. The HQN editor did her best to keep me from fainting on the other side of the table, or throwing up onto it. She patiently watched me babble and drool all over myself for about 3 of my allotted 8 minutes. Then she leaned forward and said, "Look. I know you're nervous. But just take a deep breath, and tell me what your book is about."

I tried. But compressing an 85,000-word book into a two-to-five-minute pitch is difficult, even for an established author. Which I definitely was not. The editor was sharp, though, and identified immediately the "hole" in my plot—at least as far as Harlequin requirements go. She explained to me what was missing, how I might fix it, and left me with a hearty handshake, a smile, and wishes for much success.

I went back to my hotel room, threw up my lunch, and then cried for two hours. I called my husband and swore I was done with this writing game. I just couldn't do it. I wasn't good enough, and had no idea how to *get to be* good enough to make the grade.

After imbibing in enough white wine—in this case, more accurately spelled w-h-i-n-e—I passed out and woke up at 2 a.m. with a dry mouth, a wet pillow, and a head full of characters. They were *my* characters, and they were all screaming at me: *Get the hell out of bed and boot up your laptop! We have work to do.*

A year later, at the same conference, I pitched the same book to the editor of a small press, and came home with a contract.

In the five years since I started pitching at conferences, I've secured spots two more times (after the Harlequin pitch) to editors from major New York houses. Once, I got a "thank you, I'll be in touch." The next time, I was asked, again, for a partial—the first three chapters, along with an outline of a *proposed marketing strategy* (hmm—I thought that was *their* job).

Three months later, I received a curt rejection email from the editor.

This is the bottom line: securing a contract with a major publishing house is tough. Not impossible, because many others have done it. I have not. In retrospect, seven years into the quest and with five published books under my belt, I'm not so sure a traditional contract with a major publisher would have been a good fit for me anyway. As my tale continues to unfold, you will understand why.

Which is why you, as a writer, should decide what your pot of gold at the end of the publishing rainbow looks like. Only then will you be able to determine which avenue you should pursue.

The Numbers Game

Is it worth it? Is pursuing the big time worth the searching and the querying—and the waiting and the conference expenses and the intestinal distress and the hangover—to secure a contract with a major publisher? For some, yes, absolutely. Holding that contract in your hands is the high point of your life, rivaled only by holding your firstborn child in your arms.

Sans the stretch marks and the stitches.

Personally, I can only imagine, since it's never happened for me. But I can tell you that each and every contract I've secured with small, independent publishers felt almost this good. If I were a smoker, I'd have lit one up the minute I got the signed copy in my inbox.

"Hey," I'd mumble, swaggering, through the cloud of smoke around my head, "I just signed a contract on my book."

I said those words, but with no smoke. And mumble doesn't really describe how I said the words accurately. It was more like shriek.

Maybe I should have taken up smoking after all.

But what will you get besides a contract—*really*? Well, for one, a contract with a major publisher traditionally comes with an *advance*. This is a check, which could range from several thousand dollars to seven figures. It all depends on how much the publisher is willing to gamble on you and your book. Because basically, that's what they are doing—gambling that your book will be the next *New York Times* Best Seller. The next to garner Hollywood's attention.

If you're a newbie—a debut author—be thrilled and honored if the check has a single-digit, prime number with three zeros before the decimal point. Bear in mind, if you've secured this contract through an agent, you will not get a check for whole $2000—the agent's customary 15% comes right off the top.

Okay, so then what happens next?

Your manuscript will be due by a certain date, in the most highly polished form that you can provide, to your agent, who will forward it to the publisher. Your story will then enter the labyrinth of the publishing world, to disappear and resurface multiple times in various stages of gestation over the next 18 months to two, sometimes three, years.

The specifics of the process vary from publisher to publisher, contract to contract. Since I've never actually secured one of these major publishing deals, I can only tell you what I've heard from fellow authors who have. There will be two, three—one told me *ten*—rounds with editors who will either become your closest allies, or your most dreaded enemies. You can expect to spend many more hours on this book than you spent in the initial writing process—exponentially. But in the end, you will emerge with a polished manuscript worthy of publication under the name of whatever major house you are with.

Let me repeat that part—worthy of publication **under the name of whatever major house you are with.**

This costs you nothing. And you still have your advance—minus your agent's fifteen percent—sitting in the bank. Or at the very least, the touristy pics, souvenir trinkets, and a fading sunburn from the trip to Tahiti the advance bought for you. The publisher will format the book for you, and provide you with a cover image.

Warning: do not expect any input on what your cover looks like. For that matter, your title could and usually does change too, according to the decision of the more experienced marketing teams who work for the publisher. In all likelihood, by the time your book lands on the front table of Barnes & Noble, you won't even recognize it.

Which could be a good thing, or a bad one, depending on what your pot of gold looks like.

One thing is for certain: the only way your book *will* end up on a table in the front of a bookseller like Barnes & Noble is if your contract is through a major publisher. They own the prime real estate in the brick-and-mortar bookstore world. In most cases, the *only* way your book will make it onto a major bookseller's shelves *at all* is if your contract is with one of the Big Five.

A contract with a good, big publisher will also earn you advertising, interviews, and a generous amount of reviews—even before the book comes out. Expensive, paid reviews, like through Kirkus. These help sales numbers. They draw attention to your book and make the world believe it's the next best thing since automatic transmissions. There is no doubt: your book will have its best—*its very best*—shot at being successful. At hitting the big time. Of making your name—or your pseudonym—a household name.

But how much, in the end, will you get to take home? Can you retire? Book a luncheon with Stephen King or J.K. Rowling to discuss the authorial life?

Well, you got the advance, which is fantastic. But bear in mind, it might be the last money you see on the book. The advance is just that: an advance on future sales. You will not make another penny of royalty money until your book has earned for your publisher an amount in excess of the check issued to your agent—before their cut came out. Even then, the percentages are low: mere pennies on the dollar of the book's cover price. Sometimes, even lower.

The sad fact is that less than 40% of books contracted with the major houses actually break even. Those that skyrocket and soar, of course, make up the difference—for the publisher. But as far as your book and your career?

The Road to Publication

The good news is that no matter what, you will get to keep your advance. They don't take it back.

The bad news is that you will, in all probability, never be offered another contract on another book by that major publisher—or any of the other four.

I attended a writer's panel discussion recently where I met two fellow authors, both of whom are traveling on different roads to achieve their publishing dreams. One was contracted with a small house, the other with several, along with another contract with one of the Big Five. They both wrote different genres than I, and I got the distinct feeling they looked down on my path—not only the fact that I write romance, but that I had transitioned solely to self-publishing.

One of the authors revealed, during the lively Q&A discussion, that she has a hard time letting go of her works. She has a novel sitting in a drawer that's been complete and edited, ready to go to her agent for years. When asked why it's still there, she confessed to having a "hard time letting go."

Letting go of what? As the discussion continued, she revealed that although she is a hardcore, traditional-publishing-route kind of gal, she always writes two books at the same time: one for her agent/publisher, and one for herself. She knows that once she "lets go" of a novel, it will never be the same again. Essentially, she loses control over her work—her Word Art.

I asked the other author what his ultimate goal for his writing was, and his reply?

"I want to see my name on the *New York Times* Best Seller List."

"A noble goal, but at what cost," I asked him? "Doesn't it bother you to lose control over your creative product?"

No, he claimed. That was his goal, no matter what the cost. He told me he'd had an idea to write a particular book, and although his publisher bought the idea, they then proceeded to give him a specifically detailed outline of how the book was to be written.

"If they'll pay me enough money, I'll write it any way they want."

It works for him. The process works, evidently, for the other author as well, and for hundreds and thousands of other authors who choose the traditional route. They are pursuing their authorial pot of gold along what I consider to be a difficult, frustrating highway. Good for them. As long as they are happy with their choice, I wish them much luck, and all the success they deserve.

But keep in mind, fledgling author, there are other routes. Other ways to reach the publishing pot of gold.

The Road to Publication

Claire Gem

Your Choices—Traditional Publishing: Route B

Another, increasingly popular way for writers to achieve their goal of publication is through the small, independent publisher. Small Presses, as they are called, come in a variety of flavors. They represent the "halfway house" between the major publishing companies and self-publishing. By definition, they are companies with annual sales that fall beneath a certain figure. Do not confuse the Small Press with an Indie or Vanity Press, which are discussed in the next chapter.

Small Presses usually specialize in particular types of books, like poetry, anthologies, memoirs, or one of the many varieties of "genre fiction," i.e., science fiction, fantasy, romance, etc. There are also Small Presses who concentrate solely on what is considered "literary fiction."

If you don't have the desire, or the stamina, to try your hand at self-publishing, find yourself a small press who specializes in your genre.

I have a bit of experience with small presses, having signed contracts with four of them over the past four years. By sharing my stories of wonder and woe, I hope to give you a broad-based foundation from which to decide if a Small Press is the right route to your publication pot of gold.

My first publishing contract was with a small press who publishes both fiction and nonfiction, but has a special fondness for memoir. I had taken an online course given by one of their editors, and was impressed with her expertise and delivery of the course material. When I discovered she was also an acquiring editor for this small press, I queried her regarding my memoir, a manuscript which also comprised the thesis for my MFA in Creative Writing from Lesley University.

Three months later, I held my first, official contract in my hands.

It was a special day, indeed. Torn between jubilation and disbelief, I think I printed off the contract three times before I could convince myself that it was real. I ran through the house (actually, down the hall at my day job) with the printed contract waving from my fingertips. It was real. It had my name on it. As a writer, I had been, officially, validated.

From that day, to the day I held the published book in my hands, seemed to take *forever*.

It was, in truth, a long time—nearly three years from contract to publication. But working with their wonderful editor to develop my book was an enlightening, exhilarating experience. I learned how to figure out what major themes my book represented. We rearranged chapters and scenes until what started out as a nonfiction sequence of events transformed into an engrossing, emotionally poignant story. My story.

And although the publisher started out with a definite idea of what she wanted my cover to look like, she was more than accommodating in providing me with a cover I loved. Thank you, Louella Turner of High Hill Press.

Over the next two years, I secured contracts with three other small presses. Not all of the experiences were wondrous. I sparred with an editor who argued over the most ridiculous, minor points, such as my characters should be drinking coffee, and not herbal tea. Seriously. I guess since she was from Seattle, I shouldn't have been surprised, but . . . seriously? There is life after Starbucks—a company which, by the way, also produces some very tasty herbal and chai teas. (Apparently, Editor X had not noticed the tea selections.)

All three of these presses would not provide me with release dates until the books were days—in one case, hours—away from publication. How can one build a stir, plan a Facebook launch party, or do any kind of pre-release hoopla with no notice?

I had no input on the cover images of any of the other three books. Two provided me with decent covers—at least, ones that I was comfortable with. The other published my book—without my knowledge until after the fact—with a cover image I was embarrassed to admit belonged to my book. I got an email at 5 a.m. one morning—

"Oh, by the way, your book has been published and is now live on Amazon as well as sites X, Y, and Z. Attached is the cover image."

It was the first time I'd ever seen the cover image. Yikes.

One book came out with so many copyedit oversights that I had to threaten with action from a literary attorney to have corrections made.

However, one of the editors I worked with was so amazing, and helped me so much to improve my story, that I will continue to hire her services as a freelancer to edit my self-published books. Thank you, Joanna D'Angelo.

And about the money . . . what money? That's about what it comes down to when you are dealing with a small press. Don't get me wrong—they give you a LOT, at no cost upfront. Editing (for better or worse), a cover image (ditto), formatting, and publication in digital and print-on-demand formats. But I'm only getting 35% of the digital book price, and pennies on the dollar for the print book. One book, even though it's sold fairly consistently and has been on the market now for two years, has netted me less than one hundred dollars in royalties. In total.

I have made tons of friends through these small presses—other authors who help cross-promote each other's books, support each other through the editing process, and beta read the next work-in-progress. Many are very happy with their contracts, and have multiple books through each small press. Most, however, view their books as hobbies, and not business ventures. They must—because at the rate of royalty they're making, they'd have to have several hundred books published before they could even think of retiring to a full-time authorial life.

Unless they live in a third-world country.

The Road to Publication

Your Choices—Subsidy or Vanity Presses, and Assisted Self-Publishing

The Subsidy Press is a publisher-for-hire. Due to the negative connotation of the term "vanity," we will refer to these types of publishers here as Subsidy Presses. But there is a distinct difference between a Subsidy Press and a company specializing in Assisted Self-Publishing. We'll take them here one at a time.

The Subsidy Press

This type of company was very popular way back at the beginning of the self-publishing era, when all an aspiring author wanted was to bring their complete, formatted, PDF file to a printer and have it made into a book. A few still exist, but don't expect more from them than the simple service of printing your book. You will be required to provide them with a PDF of a complete, paperback cover (front and back), along with the formatted interior PDF file. Then, for a certain number of dollars per copy, they will produce a finished product. You walk away with a box of books. It will then be up to you to do with them what you desire: market, display proudly on your mantelpiece, or give away to friends and family.

A true Subsidy Press is simply a printing service—a glorified Staples or Office Max. They will NOT reject you (as long as you can pay for their services), and will NOT even read your book. They will simply turn the file you have provided into a printed book.

Assisted Self-Publishing

The important difference between a Subsidy or Vanity Press and one specializing in Assisted Self-Publishing is that there are gatekeepers. I had a very enlightening conversation with a representative from Authorhouse, one of the largest companies of this kind, in which he set me straight on a few points.

I was under the impression that as long as you had the money to pay them, presses such as this would not turn you away. I was wrong.

The Road to Publication

Authorhouse most definitely has submission guidelines that they adhere to, and they *will* read and evaluate your manuscript. They have standards by which they determine whether or not they will take on your project. You can find out more about their services at their website.

Authorhouse offers "publication packages," and a variety of a la carte services to choose from, which range from $899 to $11,899 (at the time of this publication). They also have a list of "add-on" services, described thus:

<u>In-store Stocking Bundle</u>

Aside from the chance to have your book displayed on shelves, you can also interact with book enthusiasts through a book signing event.

<u>In-store Stocking and Signing Bundle</u>

Ideal for authors whose goal is to explore the possibility of having their books displayed on the shelves of a local bookstore.

For Authorhouse's least expensive package, you get the editing, cover design, interior formatting, distribution, and the marketing consultation necessary for your published digital book. You also receive one paperback author copy, and three additional paperbacks. As the prices increase, so do the amenities, all the way up to the most expensive package, which includes fifteen hardcovers as well as forty paperbacks, a plethora of promotional materials (book stubs, business cards, and bookmarks), and an extensive catalogue of promotional assistance.

There are many other companies who offer similar services to Authorhouse. One simply has to do an Internet search. The main differences to be aware of, when it comes to evaluating these companies, is the level of rights ownership. Some presses retain some of the rights (for example, control over distribution), while the author is the only one who has taken any sort of financial risk.

A dear friend of mine—we'll call him 'Mark'— had been dreaming of writing a story his entire life—one particular story, one he was passionate about. Finally, after he retired, he wrote the book. After nearly two years of disappointment and frustration, submitting to editors and agents and receiving either rejections or no replies at all, Mark sought out a Subsidy Press. His book was published with a colorful cover image, and black-and-white line drawings (of his own creation) throughout. It was a beautiful product. It was the culmination of his lifelong dream.

Mark's book never made a *New York Times* Best Seller list. It did not win any awards, though I'm not sure he even entered it into any competitions. And I'm sure the meager earnings he made (and probably still makes) off the book's sales won't buy him a beachfront villa in the south of France. But one thing is for certain: this company helped Mark reach his publication dream—his own, personal, publication goal. I don't know how much it cost him, nor do I care. The look of pride on the man's face as he gifted me a paperback copy was, obviously, worth the price of admission.

Mark will never write another book. He has no inclination to pursue an authorial life. He just wanted to tell his own, special story, and see it come to reality. It has.

Subsidy presses serve an important purpose in the work of the Creative Writer. They enable those who have a story to tell to see the dream come to fruition. If all you want out of your writing life is to hold a paperback in your hands, or to see the digital version for sale on Amazon or some other eBook vendor website, then a Subsidy Press is the right fit for you.

The Road to Publication

Claire Gem

Your Choices—Do It Yourself: The Ugly Bastard StepChild

There is absolutely no doubt: that's how most all self-published books were received, in the beginning. Self -publishing—*on your own*—was considered cheating, dodging the system, taking the easy way out. The practice was looked down upon as bad, or even *worse* than publishing with a vanity press—at least with a vanity press, you had to pay somebody to get the job done.

But the giant Amazon god, in 2007, granted the right to publish to anyone. *Anyone.* If you could type your story into a word document, save it, and hit send, you could be a published author. Essentially, for free.

Without a doubt, many of the early self-published works were less than stellar in quality. But Amazon is smart, and they're on top of their game. They figured this out quickly, and when the complaints started coming in from readers who'd paid for an eBook, only to receive an unreadable, badly formatted mess, Amazon promptly raised the bars on the gates. Now, Amazon carefully monitors the books published through KDP, and will flag and pull titles with obvious defects. Even the free ones.

So, what has this done to the publishing industry? For one, it has flooded the market with reading material—a study from 2014 claimed over 5000 digital titles were added *a day*. Are they all imminent best sellers? No, of course not. But are they of better quality—at least in readability—now than they were in 2007? Yes, definitely.

What happened in the subsequent ten years is what happens, inevitably, in any "new" industry. The people who get involved, and are serious about producing a quality product, rise to the top. The rest either fall to the bottom of the silo like chaff, or give up entirely.

Is it easy? No. But it's free, right? Well, it can be—publishing through KDP Select, as well as Createspace, costs nothing, until you order that first paperback proof. But the process of getting your book into a competitively marketable condition takes time *and* money. How much depends on the route you choose. In this book, I will concentrate on the specific process necessary to self-publish a title on Amazon. A *good* book. One worth the price readers pay for it, and one with the potential for continued success.

The Basic Steps involved which will each be discussed as we proceed on our Road to Publication:

1. Write the best book you can write.
2. Find beta readers. Join a critique group. Ask for feedback. Make changes accordingly, i.e., kill your darlings. Drown your puppies.
3. Hire an editor—a real one. One with credentials and experience, preferably in your book's genre.
4. Design a Cover. This can be achieved in a variety of ways, and can cost little to nothing, or many dollars. Or, if you're a visual/graphic artist as well as a Word Artist, you may be able to design one yourself.
5. Format the manuscript. This is time-consuming, aggravating, but relatively simple once you've done it a few times. Formatting for digital and print formats is completely different. Most are better off simply hiring someone to do it.
6. Perform your Quality Control steps.
7. Choose your Search Categories. This is crucial to the book's discoverability, and chances for success.
8. Choose a release date—wisely. Books published on New Year's Eve won't have as high initial sales numbers as ones published mid-week in the middle of February. Did you know that all the large publishing houses publish *only* on Tuesdays? *Fact.* This is the basic marketing strategy: choose times when people aren't distracted by all sorts of other activities in their lives.
9. Plan your Launch—wisely. A book launch can be as simple as a Facebook party, and as complex as a catered event in a local bookstore. More on that later.

10. Hit "Publish." Voila! You're a published author, right? No. You're a published *writer*. Remember the difference between a Creative Writer and an Author? The work, my friends, has just begun.

The Road to Publication

Darlings and Puppies

No, I'm not talking about romance novels or dog stories here. I'm talking about the next part of the publication road we're about to encounter, which can be the scariest, as well as the most painful. Many aspiring authors reach this fork in the publication highway and slam on the brakes with both feet. They never work up the courage to make that turn onto the treacherous, rutted path ahead toward their dream of publication.

A frighteningly large percentage of Creative Writers never segue onto Appraisal Alley.

This is the tough part. We have a brilliant story concept, created sparkling characters. Our plot is as exhilarating as a thrill ride at a theme park. Some scenes make us laugh, others bring us to tears. Our scary parts are terrifying, and our love scenes are swoon-worthy.

Our completed manuscript is perfect. It's our baby, our unique creation. Absolutely perfect. We don't want to change a thing.

But what if nobody else thinks so?

At the novel revision panel discussion I mentioned previously, there was one attendee who timidly raised her hand and asked this question:

"What if I'm happy with my manuscript just the way it is? What if I don't want to revise it?"

The poor girl was clutching her laptop to her chest defensively, on the drive of which, I'm certain, her treasured pet of a manuscript was etched. The expression on her face allowed the onlooker to easily replace that laptop, in their minds, with either a defenseless six-week-old puppy, or an adorable infant of the same age.

I will never forget the day one of my professors at Lesley University, in the first semester of my MFA program, stood up in front of a room of thirty-odd wannabe authors and said, "Today we're going to learn how to kill our darlings. Drown our puppies."

Yikes. What the hell kind of twisted, sadistic program did I sign up for here?

The Road to Publication

This is the problem: we all, as individual human beings, wear a set of goggles. These goggles allow us to see the world from our own, unique perspective. But the lenses also tend to distort our view of reality, making them, truly (pardon the cliché), rose-colored goggles.

Let's go back to my friend Mark and his once-in-a-lifetime, subsidy-published novel. He was so terrified that someone would steal his story idea that he never let anyone else read it (except his wife) until it was published. He was even hesitant to allow the editors at the publishing house take a look until he was sure the contract protected his rights to *his story*.

Oh, it was okay if they wanted to make grammatical or punctuation corrections to Mark's manuscript. But basically, like the attendee at the revision workshop, Mark believed his story was perfect the way it was. He would allow no changes beyond those that brought it up to reasonable, English-language standards.

Many Creative Writers feel this way about their manuscripts. After all, they've spent hundreds, if not thousands of hours in the crafting—hell, most took longer than it takes to gestate a human child. Besides, man, it's art, remember? Who can define what "art" is, and who are you (or anybody else) to question or criticize my personal, unique, interpretation of how this story needs to be told?

Again, we must go back to our goals for our Word Art. Do you love your manuscript just the way it is? Then subsidy or self-publishing are your only palatable options. Because if you want your book to be accepted, either by a Big Five publisher, or by a Small Independent Press, or even by the readership of Self-Published books, you're going to have to steel your heart, seal your lips, and bring your manuscript out from its hiding place.

Let me first allay one big fear for you. The chances of someone stealing your story idea, rewriting it with a few "ands" and "buts" moved around, and making a million dollars on it, are about one in twenty-seven-million. First of all, if you scratched out a paragraph describing your story concept and passed it out to fifty different wannabe authors, they would each come up with their own interpretation of that plot, those characters. You would end up with fifty books that, although similar in concept, would ultimately be completely different.

I stated "wannabe authors" in the previous paragraph for a reason—no self-respecting, established/published author would bother stealing your story idea. They have far too many of their own waiting to be written.

And what about copyright, you ask? Doesn't U.S. Copyright protect me from someone stealing my story?

Well yes, and no. Even if you do not register paperwork (and pay for it) with the U.S. Copyright Office, once your work is fixed in a "tangible form," i.e. printed manuscript, document on a computer disk or hard drive, etc., it is technically, legally yours. No one can steal it and sell it without first seeking your permission, and without you receiving some sort of payment or royalty for the subsequent sales.

Does it happen? Yes, all the time. In this modern digital age, anyone, from anywhere in the world (even Mars, if they have Wi-Fi) can and does steal previously published manuscripts. It happens every single day. They put them up on their makeshift websites and sell them—your stories!—sometimes even with your cover image and your name on it, without giving you a dime. Can they be stopped?

Yes, and no. You can send a Cease and Desist letter, ordering them to stop selling your book illegally, and threaten them with legal action if they don't. Most of the time, the bigger, more business savvy sites will comply. But what if they're operating from some tiny island off the coast of Tipperary? Do you think they're going to worry about your attorney serving them with papers?

Are you even willing to pay a bazillion dollars to an attorney to stop the scoundrel bookseller from making ten bucks every six months by selling your book? That's up to you. I look at it this way: every time a Tipperarian buys my book from ScoundrelBookseller.com, he or she will tell three of their friends about my book. Two of them won't care, but the third one will want to read it—and doesn't trust using their credit card on

ScoundrelBookseller.com. So, they'll go to Amazon and buy it from me.

Cha-ching. Thanks, ScoundrelBookseller. You just netted me another fan.

Not to treat this subject lightly, once you do have a published manuscript out there, it's wise to set up Google Alerts for your title and your name (or pen name), so if ScoundrelBookseller.com lists your title, you will know about it—and take appropriate action. Which you should, even if it's simply to issue a Cease and Desist letter.

But I seem to have gotten off track here, while you're still sitting there clutching your manuscript to your chest, eyes round with terror. Your palms are sweating so badly the ink is starting to smear. Oh my, I'm terribly sorry. Calm down. Lay that stack of papers on your lap (face-down—I promise I won't look), and we'll talk about what you should do—what you *need* to do—in the next leg of your journey to publication.

It's called Killing Your Darlings, or Drowning Your Puppies. You choose your poison. Now I'll tell you how we go about commencing this process.

You need to put on your right-turn signal and turn onto Appraisal Alley. This is the place where you squeeze your eyes shut and thrust your precious, baby book out into the cold, cruel world of Readers. Now you'll notice I designated, specifically, *readers*. Although it can be tremendously helpful to allow other *writers* to read your book baby, there are a few, deeper ruts in this road that will reveal themselves later on. But first, I'll suggest several ways you can seek out objective opinions of your book baby.

In the beginning, when you're first learning your craft, you need to seek out readers who also know something about writing. Where?

- Local writer's groups
- Friends who are writers, perhaps through local writing chapters
- Local critique groups
- Online critique groups

Preferably, these writers also write in, or are least are avid readers of, your chosen genre. Why? Let me give you an example.

My first critique group experience, though positive, did not help me much aside from boosting my ego. Not a bad thing, but certainly not helpful in furthering my writing skills. My local bookstore holds a monthly critique group meeting. The small, cozy shop also makes the greatest cappuccino in the area, and sells new and used books as well as homemade candy, fudge, crafts, and bric-a-brac.

I was warmly welcomed on my first visit, but a tad disappointed to discover that most of the other attendees were poets. I write fiction, and some non-fiction. I was informed that there were two other members who attended infrequently, and only one of them wrote fiction.

We all settled with our steaming cups or frothy concoctions, and proceeded to pass out copies of our work, short pieces we wanted feedback on during that session. Each member then "took the stage" for twenty minutes or so to read it aloud, and then awaited feedback from the other members.

Not only do I not write poetry, but it's not really my choice of reading material, so my comments were vapid and weak at best. I soon discovered that my fellow members not only didn't read much fiction, but few read "genre fiction," and none read romance. Needless to say, although I made a number of dear friends, and actually gained a fan, over the following few months, I didn't really receive—or contribute—much in the way of useful criticism during those evenings.

My next foray into the forest of critique groups was spot-on: through a friend, I discovered an online circle that specialized in my genre. I applied and was accepted, and what followed over the next two years was the most productive education I've ever received in my pursuit of publication. Even if you count my years spent earning an MFA in Creative Writing (!)

The moderator/creator of the group organized it brilliantly. Once a month, each member would send her up to 5000 words of a work-in-progress, designating a sub-genre. If the submission was from the middle of the book, one was allowed up to 250 words (one page) to summarize the story up to that point. The moderator—we'll call her Nan—divided these subs according to genre, then sent each member two subs of genres they had agreed to critique.

We each had three weeks to complete our critiques, which had to conform to strict guidelines: comments only, no rewriting, at least two comments per page. The critique partner also had to give a one-page summary of impressions addressing specific points: conflict, plot, setting, characterization, dialogue, point of view, exposition, readability, and general comments.

Wow. This was brilliant. Each month, I read the works of two other authors—some published, some still struggling on the road to publication. In return, I received two critiques from people who read and wrote my genre. I learned so much, not only from reading the comments, but from reading other people's works. It's amazing how many times we can identify our own weaknesses in other people's writing, but can't see it in our own. I experienced quite a few "ah-ha" moments.

Alas, all good things must come to an end. Suffice it to say that the moderator of this group (who had not been, at least at that time, published) took a very personal interest in my work. Each month I received not two, but three critiques—including one from Nan herself. And she was my biggest fan until she learned that the release date for my first self-published novel was only weeks away.

I did, admittedly, ask her to read the completed novel as a beta reader. She started out loving it until about a third of the way through, at which point she began to breach her own cardinal rule: She started rewriting the book, her way. Words were exchanged, egos were damaged, and I left the group shortly before the book was released. My way.

Two months later the book won the New York Book Festival. We'll leave it at that.

That being said, I strongly urge you to seek out an online or in-person critique group in your chosen genre. You will make many friends, get an invaluable education, and walk away without a huge student loan payment to show for it.

This story, however, highlights one critical difference between a "critique partner" and a "beta reader." The job of a critique partner is to identify and point out possible *technical* problems in your book—**specific problems**, as in plot inconsistencies, head-hopping (confusing point-of-view changes), unlikeable characters, et cetera. You want your critique partner to *read like a writer*.

A beta reader should act the role of a reader, i.e., read the book as if they'd plucked it off a shelf at the library or at their local bookstore, then give you their overall impression. Beta readers are exceptionally good for pointing out content flaws. Examples:

- I loved it, but the hero is somewhat obnoxious in Chapter One.
- Why did the heroine do what she did on page 237? It doesn't make sense . . .
- The love scenes were too short/too long/too graphic/not graphic enough.
- Whatever happened to the heroine's Aunt Sally?

Beta Readers are the ones who will identify your darlings, and suggest you kill them. They will ferret out your puppies, and help you to drown them. It's not nearly as barbaric as it sounds. I promise.

Ironically, as it turns out, the parts of our novels that we like the best, that we think shine the brightest, usually don't belong in there. They are either unnecessary tangents streaking off from our original story line, or they simply slow down the pace. Let me give you a personal (and pretty painful) example.

The Road to Publication

At my very first roundtable workshop in my MFA program, the piece I had submitted was being "critted" around the table. The consensus was about the same.

"The last page was awesome. But the first three pages, well, they just seemed like unnecessary background story. Like throat-clearing."

Throat-clearing. That term has never left my brain, and I'll always be in debt to the critique member who coined it (damn if I can't remember her name!). She was absolutely, positively dead on. Those first, five-hundred words or so had to go. They were just leading up to the story I really wanted to tell. I was warming up. I was clearing my throat.

But those first three pages were my favorite parts! My darlings. My puppies. Please don't tell me I have to . . .

I needed to axe the darlings. Drown the puppies.

Backspace. Delete. *Gone.*

This is one of the most difficult things one can ask a creative writer to do.

I'm thinking, "What? So, who would have had the guts to tell Melville that *Call me Ishmael* was a crappy way to begin a story? Nobody, right? Who said Nabokov was simply a horny old bastard when he began *Lolita* with a line including the phrase "fire of my loins"? And why didn't somebody tell Van Gogh he'd included too many black birds in his *Field of Crows*? Bah! No wonder he never made it as an artist."

A critique group or partner is supposed to pick your piece apart, like a buzzard on roadkill. That's their job. It's your job to toughen up, decide what advice to take, and what advice you simply don't agree with, because that's okay too. Let me repeat that: *some advice you don't have to agree with, and that's okay.* Remember the editor I told you about who didn't like the fact that my characters preferred tea to coffee? Well, that sort of feedback, unless it really conflicts with the story line, should be ignored.

I dearly miss my critique partners in the online group. But when I had the falling out with the moderator, it was obvious I'd have to give it up. If things had turned out differently, I would still, even now having published a total of five books, be a member of that critique group.

That doesn't mean I don't seek the advice of beta readers. When my novel is completed, and polished as far as I can get it polished, I seek out at least two, but no more than five, beta readers. People who know, but don't necessary *love* you. Why the limited parameters? I will explain.

Finding readers who I know are fans of the genres I write is the first step. There's no sense in passing along my sexy contemporary romance manuscript to my friend who reads exclusively crime-mysteries, or the one who's into inspirational fiction. So seek out readers, either among your circle of friends, or writing groups, or online communities, who like the kinds of books you write. Ask them if they'd like a "free book," and if they'd be willing to give honest feedback.

Honest. That's a biggie here. If your Aunt Clara loves science fiction novels, and that's what you write, don't expect her to tell you the book sucked, the characters were flat, and the world you created bordered on the absurd. Unless, of course, she's like my Aunt Clara, in which case she'd let me know all of these things and more.

What you want to find is people who know you, but who aren't afraid of hurting your feelings. Your ego is going to have to don a big old suit of armor by the time your book baby is really—and I mean really—ready to dive into the sea of published novels. Because I can tell you, the readers who plunk down anywhere from a few bucks for an eBook to a twenty-spot for the paperback are certainly going to give you their honest opinion. Right there out in the open, on Amazon or Goodreads or Librarything. And by then, there won't be anything you can do to change their minds.

Why only two to five beta readers? Because things can get crazy in a big hurry. No matter how good your book is, everyone who reads it will have a different "take" on the characters, the plot, the conflict. If you get more than five opinions, you will—I promise you—get at least two people who don't hate it, but didn't love it. That will do nothing but bruise your confidence, and keep you from swinging around at the end of Appraisal Alley and heading for the home stretch. I've found, personally, three to be the magic number of beta readers.

My strategy is to "gift" the manuscript, either as a Word doc or PDF or in actual Kindle (.mobi) format (this is easy, more on this in the formatting chapter), to three readers who are willing to read my manuscript within a timely manner. Because that's the other caveat here: you don't want to hand out your almost-ready-to-publish manuscript in June and not receive feedback until October. Thirty days is a reasonable amount of time to ask anyone to finish the average length novel.

First, I ask, "I've just finished my next novel. It's a women's fiction. Would you be interested in beta reading for me?" If the answer is yes, then I ask what format they prefer, and send it off, with the specific request that they complete and send me their feedback by the same time, next month. Remind them that your editor will be waiting for the polished manuscript by such-and-such a date.

When the feedback comes in, I highly recommend having two computer monitors at your disposal, so you can keep your manuscript open on one, and the list of feedback comments on the other. Then go through, page by page, making what adjustments you agree with. Or, if they didn't give page numbers, it's simple enough to do a search for whatever sentence or phrase they are referring to.

Once your book baby has been mauled by the critique partners, then bathed and tickled by the beta readers, buckle it into its car seat. Now the search begins for your perfect editor.

The Perfect Editor

Editors, like auto mechanics, come in a variety of shapes and sizes. Each have their specialties, and most, their specific preferences. Like auto mechanics, some are certified, and some are not—although simply having that certification hanging in their shop does not guarantee the editor will have what it takes to perfect your manuscript.

Because editors are editors, not gods. What you want an editor to do is up to you. I repeat: *editors are not gods*. Ultimately, what an editor does with your manuscript is your decision, and yours alone. Here's the point at which a Word Artist needs to stand up and defend their you. Unfortunately, the route you have chosen on your journey to publication will largely determine how much control you will have over who your editor is, and what he or she will do with your manuscript.

If you have chosen the Traditional Routes, either A or B, you will be assigned an editor. This person is reputedly an expert in your genre, knows the market, and has the skills it takes to mold your manuscript into a book that will make money for the publisher. Notice that last phrase: *make money for the publisher*. The editor is not hired to admire your creative Word Art. They are not interested in preserving your unique story concept or your voice. Their job is to shape your book baby into something they believe will sell.

Even if they twist a few of its limbs out of joint in the process.

I mentioned earlier the author I met at writer's group who said she has two novels going at the same time: one for herself, and one for the publisher. She does this because she knows that once the book hits the editor's inbox, it will never be the same again. This is not always a bad thing, she conceded. Talented editors (and I've worked with a few of these myself) really know how to take a story from good to outstanding—without major reconstruction. If you are blessed to find an editor like this, grab hold, hang on tight, and don't let go. They are worth their weight in gold.

The Road to Publication

The aforementioned author also shared a tale, though, of a book she'd written addressing one, very troubling societal ill—let's say it was alcoholism—which she considered to be the theme of her book. Her editor read the manuscript and said it was brilliant, marvelous—wonderful character development, intensely emotional plot—but it wasn't about alcoholism.

"Yes," the author said, "it is. That's my theme. That's what I want it to be about."

"Well," said the editor, "we can't sell it if it's about alcoholism. So, all those scenes you wrote about alcoholism? They have to come out."

The author, begrudgingly, did as she was told. She whacked 10,000 words out of her manuscript. The entire theme, the entire reason she wrote the book, got tossed out the window. The book then became about "finding one's place in society," or something like that. I haven't read the book in either of its versions, so I can't tell you if I agree with the editor's decision or not.

YES, I CAN. I DON'T AGREE.

If the author wanted her theme to be alcoholism, why should she have been forced to abandon that swerving vehicle? Would the book have hit a bestseller list with alcoholism as a theme? I believe Chelsea Handler's book, *Are You There, Vodka? It's Me, Chelsea*, was a bestseller. But now we and the author will ever know. Because when her book baby came out, it read nothing like the one she'd labored over.

I also don't believe the bastardized version has hit a best seller list yet.

The takeaway here? Your degree of control over your Word Art will depend largely on the route you have chosen to take on your journey to publication. Undoubtedly, Traditional Routes A or B will leave you with little to no control at all. Not that it's always a bad thing: the editors could well take your manuscript which is good, but not great, and make it a smash bestseller.

Or not.

If, however, you've chosen Routes C or D, i.e. Subsidy Press or Self-Publishing, you will maintain a very high degree of control over the way your Word Art looks when it hits the sea of published novels.

For better, or worse.

With a Subsidy Press, you will still be "assigned" an editor, but since you are the paying customer, I would imagine you could argue against any major changes the editors want to make in your manuscript. Since I've never gone this route, I cannot say for sure, but I feel certain that to avoid losing your business, you might even be assigned a different editor if the relationship with Editor A isn't going well. I'm certain that editors who work for Subsidy Presses are very sensitive to the desires of their customers. Otherwise, they'd go out of business.

You might even be given a choice, with a Subsidy Press, between a "developmental" or a straightforward "copyeditor." The difference is this: a developmental editor will make bolder statements about the changes he or she feels are necessary to make your book better. This could go as far as saying "alcoholism isn't the theme of your novel," but I doubt it. They might suggest that the book may not sell as well if you insist on keeping alcoholism as your primary theme, but in the end, you are the paying customer. You will not be forced to trash your original thematic purpose.

A copy editor is more like your seventh-grade English teacher—at least, like *my* seventh-grade English teacher. Ms. Nancy Prather caught every misspelling, every misused punctuation mark, every grammatical snafu, every mismatched metaphor I could throw at her. When she got finished with my first creative essay, it looked like a two-year old had gone at it with a red pen. But she molded my essay into a grammatically correct, smoothly readable piece of English prose. That's what a copy editor will do. Most will also catch repeated words and phrases, which is a personal pitfall in my own writing.

If you have decided to go with Route D, Self-Publishing, you will need to hire an editor. But first you need to decide what kind of editor you want—developmental, or simply a copyeditor. It will cost you anywhere from two dollars a page and up, but the investment will be well worth it. At the very least, it will keep Amazon from pulling your book off the market because of complaints from buyers about "typos."

By the time I reached the point of self-publishing my first book, I already had experience with a number of editors. I knew what I was looking for, so I went shopping. And yes, you can and should shop around and "test-drive" several editors before you decide on one you commit to. As I said, it's a considerable investment—my novels, which run between 275-350 pages, cost me nearly a thousand dollars to have edited. Again, well worth the money.

Where to look? Start within your own genre, as here is where you'll find editors who "get" your style of writing. Don't choose an editor who advertises in the classifieds of a literary magazine if you write steam-punk. Go to your organization's website or local chapter's newsletters. Buy a magazine that specializes in your genre and look for ads in their classifieds. Seek out other self-published authors in your genre, and ask them who their editor is.

Treat the process just like finding a reputable auto mechanic: contact the editors—at least three—and tell them what kind of editing you are looking for. Ask if they will provide a "test-run," i.e., a first chapter edit. And what they will charge for that.

When I started out, I "test-drove" three editors, telling them I was looking for something a little more than a copyedit, but a lot less than a developmental edit. I wanted them to catch typos, misspellings, and repeated words like a copy editor, but also point out things like, "Your character's eyes were blue in the first chapter, but turned to green in Chapter Seven." Or, "You never tied up the loose end about what happened with the character's father who had the heart attack."

Trial editor number one charged me forty bucks for fifty pages and proceeded to rewrite the entire chapter, beginning to end. Her way. We both know how I reacted to that.

Trial editor number two did the first twenty pages free, caught one misplaced comma, and told me she "loved the book, couldn't wait to read more." I was looking to hire an editor, not a paid fan, so this wouldn't work.

Trial editor number three charged fifty bucks for fifty pages and caught every single typo, grammatical error, and pointed out a number of repeated words (I have my favorites, I'm sure you've noticed). I hired her.

She edited the entire book in an amazing three weeks' time, and I made my target publication date. It wasn't until the book had come out in eBook AND paperback that my audiobook narrator pointed out I'd misspelled the word "lightning." Not once, but twenty-two times throughout the manuscript.

Yikes.

I've since found another editor who I'm extremely happy with. She's like a makeup artist, touching up all my flaws without making me look more like Madonna than myself. I love her, and if you want an outstanding editor who does what we call "soft content editing," contact Allie Rottman at Silver Sparrow Editorial. She rocks—and she edited this little masterpiece as well.

So. You've gotten your critique partners' feedback, and made adjustments. You've gotten opinions from your beta readers, and tweaked the book a bit more. Your editor has sent you the final, edited version and you've either accepted—or rejected—her suggested changes. What's next?

You can't sell a book without a cover.

The Road to Publication

Between the Covers

That's really the wrong name for this chapter, because, presumably, you already have what's *between* the covers by now. What you need is the cover itself. But I got your attention, didn't I? (A little romance author's humor. Couldn't be helped.)

Again, we'll begin with Traditional Publishing Routes A and B. Your cover? Don't worry about it. You will have **no say** in what the cover looks like *at all*—unless, of course, you are as big-name as Jodi Picoult or John Grisham, and have an agent who managed to work that luxury into the contract. I did have one small publisher who allowed me to make a request as to what I absolutely did **not** want on my cover, which I did. They complied and gifted me with an awesome cover. Another publisher asked me the same question, then delivered a cover that was exactly what I said I *didn't* want—and I got to see it, for the first time, the day it was released. It had already been distributed in over a half-dozen sales channels.

I've since bought back my rights to that book.

The advice I've received from more than one published author, by both big houses and small, is "Don't even think about your cover. They know what they are doing. Let it go."

With a Subsidy Press, I believe you have more input. Again, you are the paying customer. I'm certain the author has at least the option to suggest—and receive—changes. If not an actual hand in designing the cover themselves.

If you Self-Publish, however, you have complete control over what your cover looks like. For better or worse.

Self-publishing platforms, such as Createspace and Kobo, have software tools to help you design your cover yourself. Or if you're handy with GIMP or Photoshop, you can create whatever image your heart desires, and simply upload it, print ready. Another alternative is to "hire it done." There are many artists who make it their sole business to design book covers.

A few words of warning when it comes to covers, though.

The Road to Publication

First, do your research. Google your genre, and take a look at the covers of the most popular novels. Just as with word count, the consumers of your particular genre will expect a certain "look" to the cover. If you want to attract the right readers, you'll want them to recognize your book as one in the genre they prefer.

I learned this lesson the hard way. My first contemporary romance novel, which was somewhat steamy in sexual content, had a very benign looking cover. Since the series is set on a lake, the mountain backdrop took up most of the cover, and at its base, and a lovely scene with a dock and a couple sitting side by side in Adirondack chairs on the shore. A *silhouette* of a couple. A silhouette that showed them sitting close, but definitely not in a passionate embrace.

A silhouette when, once printed, came out so dark that all you could see was the outline of their bodies. At first glance, you couldn't tell what it was. And then you saw it: a pregnant gorilla sitting in an Adirondack chair.

This was a disaster on several levels. Yes, I wanted the image to tell the reader that this was a lakeside series. But there was nothing—absolutely nothing—on the cover that indicated this was a steamy romance novel. Second, once you saw the silhouette as a pregnant gorilla, you couldn't unsee it.

It didn't sell well. And although it didn't receive any negative reviews, I believe that readers expecting more of a sweet, summer romance (or a story about a pregnant gorilla) were simply too embarrassed to post one. The cover is now changed, and while the lovely lake scene remains, a kissing couple now graces the top third of the image. Sales have improved considerably—the readers now know, from the minute they pick up or click on the book, that this is a romance novel.

Another consideration for your cover choice, especially in today's digital age, is how the image will look when shrunken down to thumbnail size. Let's face it—for most shoppers, that's how it will appear, in a long list of other thumbnail covers, until they click on it.

You want your cover to stand out, but not in a garish way. Be sure the design remains recognizable once it's reduced in size.

Consistency between covers, if you publish multiple books, is also important to establishing your *author brand*. We'll discuss that term more later, but you want people to immediately recognize a book as one of yours. Even though I write in two different genres, my cover artist (who also happens to be my sister) maintains the same overall "pattern" for the books: title at the top, author name at the bottom. The font of the titles change, but not the font of my pen name.

If you're designing your own cover, feel free to use stock photos—**royalty-free** stock photos, those that you secure either through free sites like Pixabay, or purchase from sites like Depositphotos. This is extremely important, because you don't want to get served with papers from an attorney somewhere down the line. Be sure the image you choose is royalty-free for **commercial use**. Check the distribution rights carefully for the site you choose, and be sure that use of the photo is royalty free for book covers.

And for heaven's sake, if you decide to go with a stock photo, make it your own! I've seen at least three covers of western romances with the identical picture of the same shirtless cowboy wearing the same hat—just in different colors. This is not cool. Do something different, and if you're not savvy enough with Photoshop or GIMP to do it yourself, hire yourself a cover artist.

It's not fair, but it is true: a book is judged by its cover. At least, until the reader hits "Buy Now" or carries it up to the register at the front of the store. But this is not an easy process, nor am I an expert in creating covers. I advise you to either hire a cover designer or learn the ins and outs of the following programs.

Createspace has its own nifty software program for creating a cover. If you go to their website, https://www.createspace.com/Products/Book/CoverPDF.jsp, you will learn all of the details to create and/or upload your own book cover. For your barcodes, Createspace also has several options: they will provide you one for free, but then the publisher of record will be

Createspace Independent Publishing Platform. Remember what I said earlier about this labeling your book as SELF PUBLISHED. Again, there is no longer any shame in this, but there is a stigma. I personally prefer NOT to make this information obvious.

So, for $99, you can buy a Custom Universal ISBN from Createspace, and use whatever imprint name you like. This is definitely a bargain, since Bowker, at http://www.myidentifiers.com, charges $125 for a single ISBN. I personally chose to purchase a block of ten ISBN numbers (since I knew I would be writing more than one book) for $295 from Bowker.

As for Barcodes (which you will need for your paperback book), you can either pay Bowker an additional $25 for a barcode to go with your ISBN ($150 total), allow Createspace to add a free barcode, or go to Bookow at https://bookow.com/resources.php, and they will generate a free barcode for you. Bookow also has its own cover generator, which I've heard is somewhat more precise in generating spine width than Createspace. But this is as far as I will go in trying to teach what I don't know how to do.

I have shared information about only what I have had successful experience with, so please be aware that there are many other platforms, including NookPress, Kobo, Bookbaby, etc. with which you can create covers, achieve interior formatting, and self-publish your book—either for free or with paid help. I suggest you shop around and determine which route you are most comfortable with, and go with that.

Claire Gem

The Road to Publication: Part II
A Guide for the Self-Published Author

We will now go on to discuss all of the things you will need to know how to do—or to hire done—if you decide to brave it on your own and produce an Ugly, Bastard Stepchild. Why would you do this? Let me explain why I did.

I admit it—I'm a control freak. Arguing with an editor (one I did not hire) over coffee or tea was aggravating. Having no input on my cover image was infuriating. Not seeing my own book cover until *after it was published* was absolutely absurd.

I'm not only a control freak, but I'm not particularly patient, since I'm no youngster. I would like to be able to retire to write full-time before I'm too old to remember why I started this whole journey in the first place. Which is why, in early 2016, I turned to self-publishing.

My Word Art is *mine*, so I believe it should reflect my talent, my style (again, for better or worse). I don't want to be told what my characters' beverage of choice should be. Cover image? That should not only reflect my input, but be approved by me *before* publication.

And I want to know, right down to the day on the calendar, when my book is being released. I am a firm believer in "building a buzz," pre-release. I love holding Facebook Launch Parties. I have even arranged in-person launch parties at small local businesses, complete with wine and cheese.

Control over my product is very important to me. Which is why, on April 1st, 2016, I birthed my first Ugly, Bastard Stepchild. The same one that was named a winner in the 2016 New York Book Festival competition.

Did it come free? No, though in many ways, I am lucky. My sister is a graphic artist—and an extremely patient, indulging sister. She designs my book covers. The cover for my first self-published title won the Authorsdb Annual Cover contest, as well as the NY Book Festival title.

The Road to Publication

Editing? I had to pay for that. It's not cheap, and it does take a bit of searching. I test-drove a number of potential editors before I found one who was a good fit with my genre, my voice, and who was willing to edit my book without trying to rewrite it, her way. Or one who hated tea.

But then, I've already told you about my wonderful editor.

We'll discuss one of the most important aspects of producing a self-published book—Quality Control. We will also talk about developing an author platform, and the dreaded "M" word (marketing). Naturally, if you self-publish, *all* of this will be up to you. But the rules of today have changed for the traditionally published as well. Now, even if you're signed on by one of the Big Five, they will ask you to (and expect you to carry out) your own part of the marketing for your book.

In most cases, the much bigger part. So even if you have decided to go with Traditional Publishing, I strongly recommend you read on.

These next few chapters deal with the semantics of getting your publication-ready manuscript in the shape that it needs to be in order to produce a high-quality, professional-looking book—either in digital or print. We will take each process one step at a time.

Claire Gem

Quality Control—After the Editor

If there is only one thing that you get out of this section on producing your own self-published book, I hope it will be this: Quality Control should be your #1 Priority. There are simply too many hundreds of thousands of self-published books out there with crappy editing and formatting. And this is not even considering content.

So, the last thing I want to do is to encourage the production of one more crappy, self-published book. And let me clue you in—just because you pay for a professional editing job, even with a great editor, that doesn't mean there won't be typos, missing words, repeated words, and formatting snafus in your final product.

This is not your editor's fault. When you got that edited manuscript back from him or her, you made suggested changes that you agreed with, right? Well, when you did, unless you sent the edited manuscript *back* to the editor for yet another round, there will be errors. We are all human, but our eyes don't believe it. They do us this little favor of automatically correcting every boo-boo we make so that our eye skims right over it.

Your readers won't be so accommodating.

I will share my process for Quality Control on my own books which, I'm sure, still doesn't produce a 100% perfect book each and every time (I'm sure there will be readers out there who will email me to point out such errors in *this* book). But it's my best shot, since I cannot afford two or three rounds of professional editing. And I'm also the kind of writer who insists on making those last, few little changes just before I hit "Publish." Not always perfect changes.

First, finish the manuscript. Lay the book aside for at least a week, maybe two. Allow your brain to forget every little phrase you wrote. Then pick it up again when you have a BIG chunk of time. The reason is this: You want to do that final read-through as much in one shot as you can. This will allow you to catch big, overall plot discrepancies. Things such as faulty time shifts or loose plot threads—you know, the "Whatever happened to Aunt Sally" threads.

The Road to Publication

Once you've read the book through, beginning to end, in as short a time as possible, send it off to your editor and mix yourself a cocktail.

When the book comes back from the editor, set aside another BIG chunk of time when you can do the majority of the edits in one or two sittings—same reasoning as before. Then mix yourself another cocktail, because editing, in plain English, sucks. It's like somebody pointing out the smudge on the interior of your windshield when you've just finished putting a two-hour spit-polish on your car. It sucks, but it has to be cleaned up, or the job won't be perfect.

After the editing is complete, I suggest you move on to the formatting section (which follows), because some things will jump out at you while you are performing this task that might not have otherwise.

All formatted? Good. Now upload your manuscript to whatever platform you have chosen—let's say it's Amazon, which would be Kindle Direct Publishing for digital, and Createspace for paperback (I understand the two are now linked, but that's a relatively new feature as of the publication date of this book). In any case, once uploaded, Amazon will do a quality check of their own, and let you know when a digital proof is available. Launch the digital proofer, or download a PDF of your book.

Now, set aside another large chunk of time and mix yourself yet another cocktail—you're going to want to read your book again, start to finish—OUT LOUD. Yes, you heard me correctly—out loud, as though you were reading the story to a friend. You will be amazed at how many errors, typos, missing words, repeated words, awkward phrasings, and the like your eyes won't see, but your ears will hear. Even if the words are coming out of your own mouth.

Thank you, Debbie Gilbert of Soul Mate Publishing, who gave me this advice several years ago. I didn't believe her at the time, but I sure do believe her now. Thank you, Debbie.

I've actually lost my voice reading one of my 349 page books out loud to the two tanks of angelfish in my office—in one weekend. But I caught more errors than you would believe (the fish never bothered to point out any to me, selfish creatures). It was well worth the sore throat.

When my book is going to come out in paperback, I take this one step further. I order a PROOF copy of the paperback, have it shipped Priority, and then sit down and read the book as if it had been written by someone else. There is something about your book, in paperback print format, that somehow makes it seem like "not yours." Like somebody else wrote it. These are the eyes you must see your book with before you will be able to catch as close to 100% of the errors as humanly possible.

You may also, for the first time since writing THE END, enjoy your own story. Strange, but true. I actually get anxious, wonder what will happen next, and cry at the end when I'm reading the paperback—and I wrote the damn thing!

The Road to Publication

Formatting: Digital

Let me start out this chapter with a disclaimer: I am NOT a formatting expert. What I've learned, I've learned through the school of hard knocks, along with some help from some wonderful ladies from a group called the Marketing for Romance Writers Group. If you write romance, look them up on Facebook. If you don't, there are similar groups on LinkedIn for authors of other genres you should look into.

When it comes to eBooks, there are multiple formats supported by many different devices. Amazon's Kindle uses .mobi, Barnes & Noble's Nook uses .epub. There are also about another dozen formats ranging from AZWZ to LIT to PDB, and it would be impossible here to describe the process by which one would convert their manuscripts into all of these formats effectively.

Fortunately, there's Calibre. This is a wonderful, FREE software program, available for MAC as well as PC that converts your manuscript into whatever format you need. Remember when I told you it was easy to provide your beta reader with a .mobi file to read on their Kindle or Kindle app? It *is* easy, with Calibre. Once you clean up your .doc or .docx manuscript, import it into the software, and choose whatever format you wish to convert it to. This works wonders when you want to send out the manuscript to beta readers or advance reviewers if they want to read the book on whatever device they are using. Just ask what format they need, convert, save to your computer (Calibre calls it "save to disk"), and send away.

But before you do anything with your raw, unformatted manuscript, you'll need to clean it up.

The conversion process to any of these formats can result in odd blips if you don't, and you'll have extra spaces, chopped up sentences, and other weird visuals that Amazon, in particular, will nail you for. They want a clean read for their buyers. It's really a quite simple process to give them one.

The Road to Publication

If you have created your manuscript in Word, then the file format you will be starting with is either a .doc or .docx, depending on the version of Office you are using. Even if you have written your book using a software program such as Scrivener (it is very economical to purchase, and is a marvelous tool that I simply haven't had the time to figure out), you can still export those files into a .doc or .docx format. I suggest that's where you begin.

But first things first—back up your work. Make a copy of your manuscript, and name it "original" or "backup," and save it separate from the file you are working with. This way, if you screw up, you can always delete that copy and make a fresh copy from your un-screwed-up original.

While we're on that subject, by the way, you should be backing up your work regularly, as you produce your manuscript, in some permanent way. Either periodically save to an external drive, a USB drive, a cloud, or subscribe to an automatic, remote backup service such as Carbonite. I had a nightmare experience with my first self-published book when its completion just happened to coincide with my edition of Microsoft Word deciding to die. Just hours after typing those two glorious words, THE END, I tried to reopen the manuscript to begin edits.

The 349-page Word document—all one hundred and three thousand words—opened up completely blank. Again, and again and again. Talk about aging quickly in a matter of minutes.

Thank goodness I subscribe to Carbonite, because they saved my butt as well as my sanity that day!

But back to the task at hand. Formatting, digital.

The clean-up directions I will be providing pertain to formatting into .mobi, or Kindle format. But once you have the book formatted for Kindle, it's a breeze with Calibre to convert to all of the other files except for Nook, which I will tell you about later.

Once you have the manuscript open in Word, click the Home tab, then the symbol right about in the middle of the toolbar that looks like a backwards P. That will reveal all your formatting in pretty blue backwards Ps and dots and lines. Every backwards P you see means you did a "hard return," i.e., hit the "Enter" button to start a new paragraph. But more than one of those hard returns will be seen by an eBook as something different from an extra space—sometimes an entire blank page! So, the first thing you'll want to do is to backspace and remove any extra hard returns between paragraphs, or at the end or beginning of a new chapter.

At the end of each chapter, you will want to insert a page break (except for Nook, which requires section breaks). To insert a page break, go to your last sentence and do one hard return (hit the space bar). Now click the Insert tab on the toolbar, select Pages, then choose Page Break. That will automatically bring you to a new page without all those hard returns you might otherwise have to use (which could result in a dozen blank pages in the finished eBook!)

Next, be sure you're starting out with a properly formatted design. Here are the basics:

    Font: Times New Roman, 12 point
    Alignment: Justified
    Indent: 0.3 (this should be set up in Paragraph under your Format toolbar)
    Spacing: 1.5—NO additional spaces between paragraphs
    Header/Footer: NONE, and NO page numbers

Now, here's the process to "clean up" your eBook for Kindle:

1. You must remove all the extra spaces after the periods. Click Edit, then Find, then Replace. A box will come up asking "Find What." HIT THE SPACE BAR TWICE. Then in the box asking "Replace With," HIT THE SPACE BAR ONE TIME. Now hit "Replace All"—you may have to hit that button more than once until the list under "Matches" is empty.

2. Next, you must find extra spaces after periods at the end of a paragraph that were added before you did a hard return. Go to Edit, then Find, then Replace. In the box labeled "Find What," type ^p (that's ^p with a ONE space before but not after it. My ^ is above the #6 on my keyboard). In the

"Replace With" box, type ^p (NO spaces before or after the ^p). Hit Replace All as many times as it takes until the list of matches comes up empty.

3. Extra spaces between paragraphs—these must be removed. Click Edit, then Find, then Replace. In the box labeled "Find What" type ^p (that's ^p with a ONE space AFTER but not BEFORE it). In the "Replace With" box, type ^p (NO spaces before or after the ^p). Hit Replace All as many times as it takes until the list of matches comes up empty.
4. Forced line spaces—these must be removed. Go to Edit, then Find, then Replace. In the "Find What" field, type ^l (this is a lowercase "L" with no spaces before or after). In he "Replace With" box, type ^p (no spaces before or after). Hit Replace All. It may take multiple times before the Matches box is empty, especially if you have not removed all the hard returns you made to add line spaces throughout your manuscript.
5. Tabs—Set tabs must be removed. In the "Find What" field, type ^t (no spaces before or after). In the "Replace With" field, enter NOTHING AT ALL (no spaces, nothing). Hit the Replace All button as many times as it takes for the Matches list to come up empty.

There you have it—Voila! Your manuscript is now properly formatted to upload to Kindle through Kindle Direct Publishing, or KDP, as a .doc or .docx file—except for your Chapter Headings, which now may be justified instead of centered. There may be a way to center them through Heading Styles—alas, I have not figured that out yet either. So, I simply go to each Chapter Heading, highlight it, then change the justification on the toolbar to centered rather than justified.

This is the cleaned-up file I recommend you upload to KDP for Kindle. The KDP software does an excellent job of converting this file to their particular version of .mobi. You will be able to access an online review copy, or download one to read on your Kindle or Kindle app to catch any goofs you may have missed.

Nook is a different animal altogether. If you intend to upload directly through NookPress, you will need to add not Page Breaks, but Section Breaks between chapters, or the Nook will not recognize your chapter headings. My recommendation? Upload your cleaned up .doc or .docx through Draft2Digital, and then they will distribute the file to Nook as well as a half-dozen other eBook sales channels.

But What About An ISBN?

Don't, don't, don't make the mistake I did when publishing my first eBook. I went to Bowker Identifier Services and purchased my ISBN (I actually purchased a bundle of ten because I knew I'd be writing more than one or two books). I then "assigned" an ISBN to my eBook. YOU DON'T NEED ONE FOR A DIGITAL BOOK. Amazon, or Draft2Digital, or Kobo, or whatever digital publishing format you go through will automatically (and for free) assign your book an ASIN (American Standard Identification Number). This is the only number you need to identify your eBook and secure its title with your name attached as author.

Essentially, I wasted about thirty bucks on this first book, because the block of ten ISBNs cost me $297 (in 2016). Don't make that mistake. You will need ISBNs for your print books. Save them for those.

Speaking of ISBNs and all things legal, don't forget that your book will require "front matter." This includes a title page, a copyright page (which, on the print version, must show the ISBN), a dedication (if desired), and acknowledgments (if desired).

Title Page

This can be as simple or fancy as you please, but I recommend you use a different font and larger font size for the title. Beneath that goes your author name, and beneath that, your "imprint." Bear in mind: if you publish through KDP and do not designate a "Publisher

Name," the book will appear as "Sold by: Amazon Digital Services LLC"—meaning, "Self-Published." Remember the stigma of the Ugly, Bastard Stepchild? I would rather not have my book labeled as such for all the world to see, even if there is no shame any longer in self-publishing your own books.

For that reason, I created an "imprint," which I call Erato Publishing (pronounced ERR-ah-tow). According to my attorney and tax consultant, since it's only ME that I'm publishing, I don't need to file an actual LLC or purchase a business license. I'm simply DBA "doing business as" Erato Publishing, the same as I'm DBA Claire Gem, which is a pseudonym or pen name. And for anyone who gets curious about Erato Publishing? I've purchased the domain name and maintain a very basic website through GoDaddy at www.eratopublishing.com.

Note: The laws in your state may be different. Verify with your own attorney and tax consultant before creating and using your own imprint.

So, my title pages for my eBooks look something like this:

Claire Gem

SPIRITS
OF THE HEART

CLAIRE GEM

Erato Publishing
Massachusetts, USA
www.EratoPublishing.com

For eBooks, try to keep the title page as simple as possible, because adding fancy fonts or scrollwork (like I do on my paperbacks) don't transfer well between digital formats.

Copyright Page

Next, you'll need a copyright page. Here's where you claim copyright to your work, which is legal and binding, and allows you the right to order a cease-and-desist to anyone who pirates your work (discussed earlier). You can Google various wording of copyright pages, but mine looks like this:

SPIRITS OF THE HEART Copyright©2017
CLAIRE GEM
Copyright ©2017 Frances Brown

Exclusive Cover Design ©2017 Terri DelNegro

This book is a work of fiction. The names, characters, places, and incidents are the products of the author's imagination or are used fictitiously. Any resemblance to actual events, business establishments, locales, or persons, living or dead, is entirely coincidental.

The Road to Publication

All rights reserved. No part of this publication may be reproduced, stored in a retrieval system, or transmitted in any form or by any means (electronic, mechanical, photocopying, recording, or otherwise) without the prior written permission of both the copyright owner and the publisher. The only exception is brief quotations in printed reviews.

The scanning, uploading, and distribution of this book via the Internet or via any other means without the permission of the publisher is illegal and punishable by law. Please purchase only authorized electronic editions, and do not participate in or encourage electronic piracy of copyrighted materials.

The publisher does not have any control over and does not assume any responsibility for author or third-party websites or their content.

~~~

On your paperback, your ISBN number would be inserted before the last sentence. It is not necessary for the ASIN number to appear on your copyright page for an eBook.

Dedications and Acknowledgments

These can be as simple or as elaborate as you wish, but if you do include them, be sure to place each on a separate page, and center them. Mine look like this:

Dedication

I dedicate this book, as I do all my writing accomplishments, to my husband, Clark. He tolerates my endless hours at the keyboard, listens to me spin tales over dinner and on long drives, and is, quite frankly, the reason I can write such intensely emotional romance. He taught me, over thirty-eight years ago, the meaning of . . .

~Happily Ever After~

~~~

Acknowledgments

I want to thank a very special beta reader, Theresa Flynn, who read this story in its infancy, after multiple rejections, and said, "I love this story. I cried at the end—in a good way. I just can't believe you don't have a contract on this book."

There is no better editor—no—mentor, in this world than Joanna D'Angelo. Without her guidance, this book would never have been as good as it is. And it's damn good. Better than it could have ever been without her.

~~~

Again, I highly recommend each of these, the Dedication and the Acknowledgments, appear on **their own separate page**. Some authors also prefer to place acknowledgments at the back of the book, but I suggest something else for the Back Matter.

Back Matter

The Road to Publication

Back matter is a place where you can do a little marketing, for your author brand, for your previous books, as well as for the next book you have coming out. This section is especially useful in an eBook, even more so than with a paperback, because you can include live links that will take your newly enthusiastic fan right to your website, Amazon author page, or book purchase screen.

I start out with a new, facing page after THE END, with the heading A NOTE FROM THE AUTHOR. Here I take the opportunity to speak directly to my readers, thanking them for joining my characters on their journey, and saying I hope they enjoyed the story. I also use this opportunity to remind the reader how important REVIEWS are to authors, and encourage them to leave an honest review on Amazon, Barnes & Noble, or wherever you've published the book. It helps if these links, in an eBook, are live, and take the reader directly to your book's page on these sites. But keep in mind that if you've published on Amazon, they will not allow you to include a live link to Barnes & Noble, and vice versa.

In this section I also remind the reader that I have other books available in the same genre, also live links (to the same bookseller). Don't make the mistake I have in the past, and hawk your supernatural suspense book in the back of your contemporary romance. I actually lost a few newsletter subscribers that way, with emails saying they were only interested in the kind of book they'd just finished reading.

Additionally, it's always nice if you give the reader a sneak peek into another book. You can do this by including the first chapter of your next book in the back (which costs you more pages), or you can set up an Instafreebie link to the first chapter which provides them access to the free chapter if they sign up for your newsletter.

Formatting: Print

Formatting a print edition is completely different from formatting an eBook, and since I only have experience with Createspace, that's the only instruction I'm qualified to give. Other formats may be simpler or more complicated—I don't have a clue. But I've had excellent experience with Createspace, so I highly recommend them. The product they produce is clean, professional, and consistent—the majority of sales income I make is from selling paperbacks, in person, at book signings and launch events (more about that later). So, I've handled hundreds of the books turned out by Createspace, and have had no complaints yet.

But if I did, Createspace also has a phenomenal customer support team. No waiting on hold for hours or speaking with a recording device. They have an option for *them* to call *you*. You type in your number and click "Call Me," and before you can pick up your phone it's already ringing. I've had to contact them a number of times for questions, and they have always handled my issue immediately, professionally, and courteously.

The most common size for printed paperbacks (other than the smaller, pocket-size utilized by some of the trade publishers) is six by nine inches. This is a nice, substantial book that feels good in your hands, gives plenty of room to show off that lovely cover you've created, and lots of space on the back for a blurb, author info, or even quotes from advance reviewers. That's also where the bar code for your ISBN will go, as well as your price, if you choose to put it there. I personally do not, because although my paperback novels sell for $13.99 on Amazon and Createspace, I sell them at signings for a flat $15.00 (as I mentioned earlier, my novels range from 275-350 pages, so this is a fair price for a book of that size). This covers the cost of shipping (which I pay) and makes cash exchanges easier (no pennies to deal with).

Besides, the buyer is getting an autographed paperback. And they get to meet meeeeee!

The Road to Publication

What I will provide for you here are directions for formatting a 6 x 9-inch paperback. Bear in mind: I'm sharing some pretty hard-earned knowledge! I struggled with this process ad nauseum not only for my first book, but for my second and third (until I got smart enough to type up a cheat sheet). Here's my cheat sheet for formatting the interior.

Start with a Word .doc or .docx—your finished, edited, ready to print novel. To set the size for 6 x 9, which does not appear on your list of Sizes, click on the top toolbar Format, then Document, then Layout, then click Paper Size. It will then give you an option for Manage Custom Sizes. This is where you can designate you want your document to be 6 x 9 inches.

Now click Edit, Select All, and then put in these settings:

Spacing:	1.5	
Paragraph Indent:	0.3	
Margins:	Custom	
Top:	0.75	
Bottom:	0.8	
Outside:	0.75	
Gutter Position:	Left	
Gutter:	0.13	
Mirrored:	Checked	

Go to Header and Footer and set these to:

Header from Top:	0.6
Footer from Bottom:	0.7

Page Numbering: This is tricky. If you don't separate your front matter (Title Page, Copyright Page, Acknowledgments, Dedications) from page One of the book, there will be numbers starting on the Title Page. You must insert a Section Break at the end of your Front Matter. Then click on Footer *after the start of your Chapter One.* You will see that it says Footer, Section 2. Now go to the toolbar and uncheck the box that states "Link to Previous." This will separate the page numbering and allow you to make the first page of Chapter One the actual page number one.

For the header, you can choose to either have it blank, have your author name displayed, the title of the book, or both. I have my author name on the odd pages, and the book title on the even pages. To do this, click header *after the start of Chapter One* (again, you don't want the header to appear on your Front Matter pages). Header Section 2 will appear. In the toolbar, click on Different Odd & Even pages. I then type in Claire Gem on the odd pages, and the book title on the even pages. Then either click Close Header and Footer, or double click on your text body, and voila! Your header is set.

I find that I like a little more space between my header text and the first line of text in the book, which is easy. While in the header, simply hit the space bar after your title or author name, and it widens the header one space, leaving a little extra room before your first line of the actual novel text.

Now a little more about your Title Page. This can be as simple as your eBook format, but I like to get a little fancy with my paperbacks. So, I add scrollwork underneath the title, along with my imprint emblem, so it looks like this:

The Road to Publication

SPIRITS OF THE HEART

CLAIRE GEM

Erato Publishing
Massachusetts, USA
www.EratoPublishing.com

    This is easy to do, but tricky without these few little tips. First, locate your scrolls (I purchased mine from Depositphotos. Remember to ONLY use royalty free designs unless you've paid for the right to use them!) You will need an image, which these are considered to be, in 300 dpi, not 72 dpi. Purchase the smallest size you can in 300 dpi, and save as an image.

Now, the tricky part: *you cannot copy and paste* the image into your document. Createspace will not recognize the image and you'll get all kinds of weird html symbols instead of your pretty scrollwork, or whatever design you choose. You must place your cursor on the title page where you want the image inserted, then click Insert from the toolbar, then Picture, then Image from File. Choose your design, and insert. The image can then be resized with the handy little squares on the corners, and centered with the alignment tool on the Home tab.

That's it! Easy peasey, and your book looks like it rolled off the production line of any big publishing house. In some cases, even better. I recently picked up a paperback by one of the major N.Y. houses and attempted to read it, but because the gutter was too narrow (the space between the text and the binding), I couldn't open the book wide enough to read it easily without breaking the spine. I put it back on the shelf and chose another.

This system for formatting, at least for the 6 x 9-inch size book, will produce a professionally rendered book that is comfortable to hold and easy to read.

A word about fonts: for your eBook, the recommended font is Times New Roman, 12 pt. This is the font that converts easily along a multitude of eBook readers. But for a paperback, the font choice is up to you. I've experimented with a few, but finally chose Georgia, 11 pt. as my favorite. It's easy on the eyes, large enough to read easily, yet keeps the page count to a reasonable number. For Chapter Headings, I use a 14 pt., fancier font, but for the basic novel text, it's Georgia 11 pt. for me.

I also insert a decorative scroll under my THE END, as well as beneath my Back Matter entitled A NOTE FROM THE AUTHOR. It just makes the book appear more professional, like someone—that would be you—took the time and trouble to produce a book that's not only well-written, but also pretty.

A few little side notes: I recently picked up a paperback from a traditional publisher where the copyright page was on the inside of the front cover. The inside of the front cover??? You mean they couldn't give me one extra page in this book for the copyright to have its own page? True, the more pages your book has, the more it will cost to print, but seriously? Many also have the title page on the facing page, the copyright on the back, the dedication on the next facing page, the acknowledgments on the back. Okay, so you've got only two pages to pay for instead of four. But I think it looks much more professional to have these on their own, facing page.

When you open one of my books, the first page is the title page (where I autograph the book at signing events). The back of that page is blank. The next facing page is my copyright page, also blank on the back. Then there are two additional pages, one for the dedication, one for the acknowledgments, both blank on the back. This way my first page of the book is the facing page, as it should be.

I also go through and ensure that the beginning of each new chapter begins on its own, facing page. Yes, it costs me an additional .013 cents per page, but the result is so much more professional. I want my books to be indistinguishable from any book published by a bigger publisher. It's not that difficult to do, and it's certainly not that expensive.

Back Matter

The back matter in my paperbacks is identical to that in my eBooks, the only difference being, of course, the links can't be live. So they will have to be either typed out, or footnoted so that the reader has a reference web address where they can access the information about your other books, or your Instafreebie free chapter.

There you have it. Look how far you've come! You've written a fantastic novel, had it vetted by critique partners and beta readers, designed a jaw-dropping cover, and formatted it to perfection—in both digital and paperback formats! You're done, right? All you have to do is hit "Publish" and you're on your way to a lunch date with Stephen King and J.K. Rowling to discuss the Authorial Life.

Not so fast. You may be floating in a pre-publication euphoria, but you're going to fall through that cloud pretty quick without firm footing underneath you. Because your book is going nowhere —N O W H E R E—without an Author Platform from which to market it. That's right, I've used a dirty word: The Dreaded "M" Word, Marketing.

The Road to Publication

Get on Your Soapbox, or
Your Book Needs Wings Before It Can Fly

Or . . .how to establish an effective Author's Platform.

And yes, unfortunately, that means you'll have to learn a bit—or more than a bit—about marketing. This holds true, actually, whether you've self-published your book, gone through a subsidy publisher, OR been published traditionally. More and more these days, publishers (small and large) expect an author to have a well-established Author Platform. What the heck is that?

Are you picturing a makeshift, plywood stage with some pseudo-doctor hawking his Love Potion Number Nine from its lofty height? Well, in reality, an Author Platform is something like that, except you won't need to take a trip to the hardware store for plywood.

For all of you who have decided to go the Traditional Publishing routes, you probably need to read this part as well. The last several requests for partials I received from Big Five publishers included asking for my "Author Marketing Plan." Apparently, that's not what they get paid the big bucks for anymore. Now, a good portion of the marketing for our books, no matter WHO publishes them, is up to us.

Though I cannot—and will not—attempt to cover marketing for authors in any extensive nature in this book. That's enough for a book of its own, which will be coming soon, and you will be the first to know if you sign up for my newsletter at my website: http://www.clairegem.com. I will give you the basics, though, to get you started. Marketing is a process that, in reality, should be started months if not years before you hit "Publish." You haven't done that and you're ready to release your first book? No worries. I'll still give you a basic idea of what you need to start developing. Which means . . .Ahhhhhh!!!!! **Social Media!!!**

Love it or hate it, social media is here to stay. Every month, it seems, a new platform pops up, threatening to lure me away into its depths, never to return to my unfinished manuscript again.

The Road to Publication

DON'T DO THIS.

Pick two, or three at most, platforms that you are comfortable with, even enjoy. For me, that would be Facebook, Twitter, and Goodreads. There's also Pinterest, Instagram, Snapchat, etc., but since these are basically photo-exchange sites, I find they have a somewhat more limited usefulness for me, unless I'm doing a cover reveal. LinkedIn is great too, except that I find it geared more toward the corporate world. I suppose it will be a much better place for me to market this book, a non-fiction, how-to book.

What you want is a place to connect with other authors and readers, and to develop meaningful friendships. Anybody can hit the "Friend" button and get accepted, but it takes a wee bit more time and effort to actually have someone you've never met consider you a friend. Search for groups on Facebook and Goodreads that share interest in your genre, and join them. Read the posts and react, reply, or share. On Twitter, find the hashtags related to your genre (mine would be #romancenovels, #supernatural, and #suspense), and search posts under those hashtags. Read, respond, reply, and retweet. Be a good friend, and people will want to friend you.

A word about Twitter: I have been asked by a number of fellow authors how the heck I went from 170 (that's right—one hundred seventy) to 17.3K Twitter followers in less than two years. It's very simple—FOLLOW PEOPLE BACK.

Now all of this doesn't have to cut into your writing time, or interrupt your day in any meaningful way. Like brushing your teeth, make it a habit. I have. I spend ten minutes every morning updating my social media pages. I go to Twitter and click on "Followers," then follow back every single, new follower that doesn't have an obscene photo as their profile (I'm not following you back if I'm looking at a picture of your hoo-ha in a thong).

I then post, every morning, both to Facebook and Twitter, something that has NOTHING to do with my books. My favorite thing to share is a sentence out of my daily horoscope, the author of which I also tag in the post (Rick Levine, @astromerlin on Twitter). Or I'll post an inspiring quote. Or a rant about the crappy weather, or how beautiful the snow looks outside my window (complete with picture). It takes less than ten minutes, believe me, to show people that you're not just another author hawking their books in their face. You have a life, you have other interests, other joys and gripes in your life. You're REAL.

For Goodreads, it takes a bit more effort. I belong to a number of groups, so I leave this for lunch break or after work. I read the posts in my group, respond, or maybe I'll post a review of the latest book I've read or listened to. Again, ten minutes max. You'll still have time for that greasy burger or chicken caesar salad, I promise.

For Facebook, set up an Author page for yourself. Facebook makes it easy. Just make it a separate page from your personal page, and under your pen name (if you use one, obviously) so people get to know the Authorial "you" separate from the real "you."

I've dabbled some in Pinterest, which can be fascinating and can also turn into a labyrinth if you let it. I set up a page for my first novel with pictures (royalty-free or purchased!) of my "characters," which I think still draws some attention to this book. It is still selling with some regularity after over two years. But the time it took to find those pictures, and to set the page up, wasn't worth the effort—at least, not until I retire. If you have the time and want to do something like that, it's a fun way to draw people into the "world" of your book.

So now you have a social media presence, and people out in the great, wide world of the Internet know you're an author. They know what you write, and that you've got a great new book coming out very soon. What you want to do next is create a "buzz" about your book before it even hits the sales page. How do you do that? You start to plan your Book Launch.

The Road to Publication

Claire Gem

Get Ready for The Perfect Take-Off

Sales Categories

No matter what platform you've chosen to create your book, a successful launch can make or break the initial sales peak. For the sake of simplicity (and because it's the largest online bookselling platform around), I will be referring to Amazon as our book's launching pad.

Amazon has a very secretive rubric it uses to determine where on the sales charts your book will appear, and although a lot of it has to do with the number of sales per day, a LOT has to do with what category you've placed your book under. Book categorization is a labyrinth of its own, and my best advice to you is to take a good, hard look at the book you've written, and then skim down the Amazon categories list. Where do you think it best fits?

I came across a very nifty list of the "100 Least Competitive Amazon Kindle Categories," but unless you've written a book on Surgery > Colon & Rectal, or an International Children's Bible, this won't help you much (but it might give you some great ideas about the next book you should write). This link to Kindle Direct Publishing's list of Categories can, however, be extremely helpful in allowing you to choose the category where readers will be looking for YOUR kind of book, and where they can most easily find it. This is extremely important, because with thousands of new titles being published every day, your book can and will very likely fall to the bottom of the pile, and fast. Use these browsing categories, along with key search terms to include in your book's description, to help readers find your book.

It is also helpful to search Amazon for books similar to yours—what the big publishers call "comparable titles," or "comps,"—and see what categories they are listed under. Scroll down the book's page to Book Details, and you will see the categories it's listed under. One of mine looks like this:

- **Amazon Best Sellers Rank:** #87,734 Paid in Kindle Store (See Top 100 Paid in Kindle Store)
    - #167 in Kindle Store > Kindle eBooks > Mystery, Thriller & Suspense > Suspense > **Ghosts**
    - #189 in Kindle Store > Kindle eBooks > Mystery, Thriller & Suspense > Suspense > Paranormal > **Psychics**
    - #720 in Kindle Store > Kindle eBooks > Romance > Paranormal > **Ghosts**

This is somewhat deceiving, because when I listed the book for sale, I was given only TWO choices of categories to list under. Apparently, after publication, Amazon's computer then locates other categories related to the book, and lists it under those as well (thank you, Amazon).

Since making the top 100 in any one category will make your book an Amazon Best Seller, you can see how important it is to choose wisely. Although my book is a romance, it would not be wise for me to keep it strictly under Romance > Paranormal and Romance > Contemporary—these categories are simply too competitive. But by placing it under Mystery, Thriller, & Suspense categories of Suspense > Ghosts and Paranormal > Psychics, I have a much better shot of hitting that top 100 Best Sellers mark.

So, be particular when setting up your sales categories, but don't feel that once you've chosen, you're locked in. Anytime you want your categories changed (as long as your book truly fits where you want to put it), you simply email KDP under their Help tab and ask them to make the change. Within a few days, the changes will be made, and you've got a fresh start toward making that top 100 Best Seller list.

Pre-Orders

Amazon has a wonderful feature called Pre-Orders for Kindle books. You can put your book up for sale before it's even finished (though I don't recommend this), but up to 90 days before publication date. Pre-order sales can be tracked through your Reports tab, and they can really build a buzz leading up to the release of your title. Plus, all those pre-order sales? They count as sales on release day. This will help your sales ranking right out of the gate. You will be required to make sure the final manuscript is uploaded at least three days before the release date.

I recommend you do NOT make the mistake I made in setting up a pre-order. The first time I put a book up for pre-order, I made it the same price as it would ultimately be on the day it went live. Look at this from the buyer's viewpoint: why should I give you my $3.99 three months before I get the book, and let it sit in your (or Amazon's) bank account, when it could be sitting in mine? I'll just wait until the release date and buy it then.

The problem is, by the release date, the buyer has found two dozen other books they want even more than yours, OR they have just forgotten completely about your book. Give them an incentive. Make the pre-order book a bargain: if you pre-order before the scheduled release date of April 1st, you'll pay only .99 for the same book that will be $3.99 on release day! Shout this out on every social media channel you can think of, and you will get pre-orders. And then, on release day, you've already got a nice leg up on the sales ranking.

Launch Parties

You don't need to have a paperback book in hand to throw a launch party. First of all, Facebook has a very nifty feature that allows you to create an Event (free), and invite people to attend your release party. Set a date (the day the book comes out is best), choose a really, eye-catching image for the event page (again, make sure it's royalty-free), and invite all your Facebook friends. Invite them to invite their friends. Go onto Goodreads, and let all those relevant groups you've joined know that you're holding a Facebook Launch Party on such-and-such a date, and ask them to bring friends.

This is the way I've done my most successful Facebook Release Parties: I set up the event, choosing a time slot that works over many different time zones. Remember, just because it's noon here doesn't mean it's noon in the UK, or Australia, or California. I've found the most effective (and convenient) time slot is 12 p.m.-9 p.m. EST. A start time of noon translates as follows:

AU time: 8 p.m. (previous day)

UK time: 5 p.m.

PST time: 9 a.m. (but it will run until 6 p.m. their time)

So, what are you going to do for nine hours on Facebook??? You're going to invite co-hosts to join the party and hawk their wares as well. Set up an Excel sheet, and announce on Facebook or Goodreads or in your Yahoo Groups of author friends that you're taking 30 min. time slot appointments. Keep two or three for yourself, usually at the beginning, middle and end. Be sure to have plenty of pre-written posts and neat pictures or fun games to share not only during your own time slot, but for the inevitable empty slot where someone forgets or can't make it.

Authors love this kind of stuff, and if you run a few giveaways (Facebook frowns on the term "giveaway," so use "door prize" or something like that) for a free eBook or Amazon gift card, people will flock to your party. Not only authors, but *readers*, which is who you're trying to reach anyway! Most authors who sign up for a free slot are more than willing to donate a freebie for the exposure. To keep it simple, be sure *they* are responsible for picking their winners (from those who respond to their posts or answer trivia questions, for example) and then post their winners names the next day on the party page.

Although I haven't seen a ton of sales from these FB launch parties, I definitely have gained many more followers for my author page, and lots of new names on my newsletter list. Every new "friend" you make on Facebook, especially during a book launch party, is a potential new fan for your books.

So, what about in-person launch parties? True, it's much easier to set these up once you have paperbacks in hand. But for my debut novel, I actually held a launch party for the eBook. Here's how it worked:

An author friend of mine owns a New Age Shop, and my book was a Supernatural Romance. We set a date, and I provided the refreshments—boxes of wine, jugs of lemonade, iced tea, and water. Paper cups, plates, and napkins are way cheap at the Dollar Store. I paid my friend's postage for her monthly postcard she sends to all her customers (about $80), and she featured my Launch Party on the card.

I brought my laptop and had the book trailer playing on an endless loop, interspersed with advertisements for the shop and its wares. We munched, drank, and laughed from 6-6:45 p.m., at which time I did a brief reading from the book. Then at 7 p.m. sharp, we encouraged everyone who intended to buy the book to purchase it from their digital device: phone, iPad, or Blackberry. After the buying frenzy was over, I distributed "limited edition," autographed souvenirs—the first page of the manuscript, printed on nice, cream paper and sandwiched between clear sheet covers.

The event was tons of fun, and even though it was held on the very coldest night in February the day after a hellacious snowstorm, I consider it a success. I didn't make the top 100 on Amazon, but I gained fans and more friends who will tell their friends about me and my book. All told, I think I spent about $125. It was well worth the money. I sold quite a few eBooks that night, and those who attended and who *didn't* read eBooks all bought paperbacks once they came out.

Although I make only about $2 on an eBook, I make about 5 times that amount on a paperback. It doesn't take long to make back your investment, and *gain fans*—fans who will be waiting anxiously for your next book to come out.

Book Signing Events

This is, admittedly, my very favorite aspect of the Authorial Life. I *love* book signings, and have gotten pretty good at getting them scheduled and pulling them off in a big way. Don't think that the only place a book signing can be a success is at a large retailer like Barnes

& Noble. Sad to say, the very poorest turnout and sales I've ever experienced was at the one signing I did at a very large B&N, in Tampa, FL. And it wasn't a sub-zero, February night after a snowstorm.

The key is to think outside the box. Of course, start with your local, privately owned bookstores. These small business owners are always looking for new ways to bring in business, and you can be their ticket. Saturday afternoons work best, and most owners are willing to send announcements to the local newspapers, and feature the event in their mailings and on their websites. Many charge a fee: my local store charged me $25 for my first event, but I've held a half-dozen events there since, and I've brought in so much business that they haven't charged me this flat fee since. They do take a percentage of the sales, usually 20-25%. But they handle the sales, take the credit cards, etc., so it's well worth the price.

Bookstores, though, are only the beginning. I've held signings at libraries, a museum, a gift shop, a pub, even on a dinner cruise ship on a lake! The key is to find common ground. Market in your niche. Here's how.

- Remember the friend with the New Age shop who hosted my first eBook Launch? Well, she's more than happy to host a signing for any of my supernatural suspense books.
- People love to meet a "hometown author." Contact your local library and ask if they would be willing to host a signing for you. You can offer to donate a copy to their collection—there's automatic advertising right there.
- Where is your book set? Most of mine are set in various locations in New York State, where I grew up. I've done a signing at the library in the town where I graduated high school.
- Another, extremely successful signing took place in a teeny, tiny museum in the teeny, tiny town of Loch Sheldrake, N.Y. where my first Haunted Voices book was set. The museum was thrilled my book brought attention

to their floundering tourist trade. It was so successful that I was invited back by the local pub to do another signing three months later.

- One of my series takes place on Lake George in upstate New York. Believe it or not, the tourist village does not have a bookstore, and the library did not seem interested in hosting a signing. But I did not give up. I ended up landing a signing at the gift shop owned by the scenic lake cruise company, and then did a very successful signing later that evening onboard the ship!

How does one land these events? Start with email. If that doesn't work, send a letter (not everyone, especially in rural areas, embraces the new age of the "Net.") Pick up the phone and call. Highlight the fact that your book takes place right there, in *their* hometown, and will bring attention to their corner of the world. And if all else fails, show up on their doorstep with your paperback in hand, your laptop at your side, and show them your book trailer.

Book trailers

Which, by the way, you absolutely *must* have. Book trailers, like movie trailers, are the hors d'oeuvres that whet your readers' appetites. They're way better than the blurb on the back cover, because a book trailer appeals to more than just one sense: not just words, but pictures. Not just silence, but music. And a properly produced book trailer will leave the audience hanging, so they can't possibly *not* buy the book and find out what happens next.

I will not try to teach you how to produce a book trailer in this book, nor in any other. It's truly an art, and there are many different ways of doing them. There are lots of artists who will be happy to charge you a fee for producing one for you (including me). I do recommend, however, that you limit the trailer to no more than 1 minute 30 seconds long—a minute to a minute 15 seconds is best. Be sure you (or whomever is producing the video) uses royalty-free photos, video, and music.

The Road to Publication

I can honestly say that my debut book continues to sell fairly consistently after two years, with little effort from me, simply because of the awesome book trailer that I have posted on my Amazon Author page. Book trailers sell books. Make one, or hire it done.

Press Releases

Another crucial tool you need to market your book—and to hold successful signing events—is to learn how to write an effective press release. This is a public announcement that you send out (via email and/or letter) to newspapers and radio stations local to the area where your event will be held. Here's what one of mine looked like:

Claire Gem

Erato Publishing

FOR IMMEDIATE RELEASE:
CONTACT: Claire Gem, 813.466.0886
Email: gem.writer@yahoo.com

http://www.eratopublishing.com
http://www.clairegem.com
http://www.emotionalcontemporaryromance.com

NEW YORK NATIVE SETS ROMANCE SERIES IN LAKE GEORGE, N.Y.

LAKE GEORGE, August, 2016 – Award winning author and New York native, **Claire Gem**, will be visiting the area during the Adirondack Nationals Car Show, September 8-11. The author of the first *Love at Lake George Novel*, **A TAMING SEASON,** Ms. Gem will be available for book signings on Lake George Steamboat Company's Lac Du Saint Sacrement Dinner Cruise on Sept. 9th from 6-8 p.m.

Gem, who writes both contemporary and paranormal romance, is the award-winning author of four novels. Her debut romance, "Phantom Traces," was released from Soul Mate Publishing in 2015. "Hearts Unloched," set in New York's Loch Sheldrake, was released in March of 2016 and was named award winner in the 2016 New York Book Festival Competition. Gem's other award-winning novel, "The Phoenix Syndrome," is scheduled for release September 29th.

Set in Lake George, A TAMING SEASON is the story of Zoe Anderson, a Manhattan domestic violence counselor who is trying to rebuild her life after tragic events left her a widow with scars, both physical and emotional. So she's headed back to her childhood vacation paradise, the family cottage on Lake George, which she just inherited. What she finds is a rundown shack.

The neighboring resort mogul, Jason Rolland, whisks in to her rescue, insisting Zoe stay at his upscale Lakeview Lodge. The wealthy, handsome bachelor is relying on his playboy reputation when he sets his sights on Zoe, not only for another summertime fling, but hoping he can talk her into selling her property. He's been trying to buy the eyesore next door—and raze it—for years: the last reminder of his own tragic childhood.

A TAMING SEASON is the first of what will comprise a loosely related series of contemporary romance novels set in and around Lake George Village.

Gem is available for interviews and appearances. For booking presentations, media appearances, interviews, and/or book signings contact gem.writer@yahoo.com.

~~~

    Print this release on a single page and either attach it to an email to the news and/or entertainment editor of the newspaper in your signing's location.

    And you can see here how having that imprint name and logo make it look so much more official than just saying, "Oh, gee, I have this book I self-published through Createspace . . ." First impressions matter. My signings have been featured in multiple local and regional newspapers and on websites for most of the locations where I've held signings. And I'll never forget the thrill of seeing my author name on the neon marquee in front of the Lake George Steamboat Company's docks.

    Folks love a "Meet the Author" event. I set up a simple display, depending on the genre I'm promoting that day, with little props to make it appealing. A nice tablecloth, maybe even a small, battery-operated lamp to give the table a cozy feel. A small vase with real or silk flowers. I have one neat vase my sister found that's square, and has a slot for a photo on the front—the perfect place for a miniature replica of my *next upcoming* book cover. People see it and ask, where's this book? And of course, you can tell them all about it.

For my Lake George series, my sister (who is my shopping alter-ego) found a tiny, vintage looking rowboat which you can stand on end with a shelf inside for postcards or bookmarks. She also found a miniature Adirondack chair (remember the pregnant gorilla?). Well, there's no pregnant gorilla in it, but it does make a very nice place to stack books on the signing table. For my supernatural series, I hit the after-Halloween sales to buy small ghost statues, a plaque that says "Ghost Crossing," and a small, trick-or-treat pail that I fill with mints or candy kisses.

Make your signing table fun and inviting, and you won't find yourself sitting there watching people walk by, trying to avoid making eye contact. Candy draws even the most antisocial souls. And that book trailer? I can't tell you how many books I've sold by having that trailer play intermittently on a small iPad on my table.

Money exchange? That depends on the venue. The bookstores will want to make the sale and keep a percentage. The same held true for the gift shop. But everywhere else, I took cash and credit cards (using the little Square app device for my iPhone). Price your book at an even number (like fifteen dollars) so you don't have to worry about bringing more than paper change. And sales tax? That's another thing that depends on your location, and where you live. Check with your tax consultant, and if you are obligated to collect sales tax, I recommend you figure it into the price of the book so you still won't have to deal with coin change (if the tax rate is 8%, price the book at $13.80 and it will still come out to an even $15 including tax).

I don't recommend you take checks, no matter where you sell. It's just not a smart or safe business practice in today's day and age. If they don't carry cash, they will surely have a credit or debit card they can use to buy your book, or they don't need it.

The Road to Publication

Swag

No, I'm not talking about those loopy curtains over your kitchen sink. Swag is free stuff you give away at signings, or anywhere, to promote your book and your author platform. These items can range from business cards to bookmarks to postcards to fridge magnets to . . .you name it. It all depends on how much you want to spend on something you are going to literally give away.

I've seen very clever swag, such as a plastic keychain with the book cover on it, to pretty useless, silly swag that was clearly a waste of the author's money. At one convention I attended, the "goody bags" distributed to all registrants were filled with author swag. One item was an oblong, flattened piece of plastic that looked like an oddly shaped beach ball someone had run over with their pickup truck. On the side was the author's name and the title of her book. Nobody could figure out what the heck the thing was supposed to be.

So, we asked at the luncheon. The somewhat embarrassed author explained (and demonstrated) that this was a "portable flower vase." It you pulled the flattened pieces apart and blew some air into the plugged hole (which nobody had yet found), the thing assumed an inflatable shape that would sit upright, and hold water along with several cut flower stems.

Now, I personally have never had use for a portable, inflatable flower vase, have you? Sad to say for this author, who, I later found out, spent nearly two dollars a piece on these things, this was not a smart swag investment. But I'll bet every housekeeper in the entire hotel now has one to add to the collection of oddities they've found in vacated rooms.

I started out with business cards and fridge magnets, then graduated to bookmarks, since I feel like these really get used. I've also actually sold a book or two when the person sitting next to me on a plane pointed to my bookmark and asked, "Can I see that?" Keychains, too, are useful and will attract attention, but they are more expensive. I recently got a great deal from Vistaprint on postcards. These are usually more expensive than bookmarks, but I happened to snag them on sale. A postcard can not only be used as a bookmark, but has the advantage of having room on the back for a small excerpt from your book. Cover image on the front, excerpt on the back, I ordered fifty for each of three of my books and spent less than $25 all told—shipping included.

Be watchful for sales, be smart about what you spend, and you can collect quite an assortment of useful, eye-catching swag to hand out at book signings, tack up on the bulletin board at work, or slide into the check folder at your favorite restaurant. Marketing opportunities are everywhere, if you just use your imagination.

The Road to Publication

Claire Gem

Gaining Credibility: Reviews and Contests

The best way to draw attention to your book—and to convince people to plunk down their hard-earned money to buy it—is to show that other people (other than your significant other, mother, or Aunt Sally) loved the book. How do you do this? You gain reviews, and you win contests. Sounds easy, right?

Not so much.

First of all, no matter how much readers love to read books, not a great percentage of those readers like to write about them. So even your most avid fan may not be eager, or even willing, to write a review of your book. For one thing, some readers are self-conscious, and feel they aren't good enough writers to pen a review of anything, let alone a published piece of fiction. So, give them an incentive. But how?

You could offer them a copy of the book for free in exchange for an honest review. This used to be common practice, and still is among those in cahoots with the Big Five Publishers. They distribute hundreds of free, advance review copies (called ARCs) to people in the industry they know will write a "decent" review of the book (and if they honestly can't, they won't write one that will ever see the light of day).

But if you're just starting out, and if you don't have a big publisher behind you with all those connections, how do you gain reviews?

One at a time.

There are book bloggers all over the Internet who will be willing to take a free copy of your book in exchange for an honest review. It used to be that they would be happy to post these reviews not only on their websites, but on Amazon and Goodreads as well. But in latter months, Amazon has narrowed its gates on this issue. There were, apparently, too many people either bribing or paying book bloggers (or their significant others, mothers, and Aunt Sallies) to post falsely positive reviews. For a while, the reviewers were instructed to add this sentence to end of their review: "I was provided with a free copy of this book in exchange for an honest review." But lately, Amazon has started taking down even these kinds of reviews, although in a seemingly random manner.

Bottom line is this: you're going to have to spend some money to get valid reviews. What I recommend is finding readers who are interested in reviewing your book, then gifting them the book though Amazon. Books distributed in this manner will then show up a "Verified Purchase," making them valid in the eyes of Amazon.

Problem is, the person to whom you "gift" this book might well choose to use that 2.99 credit on another book, and not yours at all. It's a sticky business, and I'm not at all sure the right answer to give you.

One tactic I have used with limited success is to distribute copies of my eBook to interested parties BEFORE the book is released, and then asked them to post reviews on the day of the release. Even this wasn't overwhelmingly productive. I gave out about 25 copies, and got 8 reviews. So far, Amazon has not pulled any of these advance reviews.

Folks just don't like to write book reviews. And honestly, with all the hoopla lately about false reviews and "paid" reviews, I'm not sure how much longer buyers' purchases will be influenced by reviews anyway.

Of course, you can always plunk down the big bucks and buy yourself a Kirkus Review. In the words of Kirkus, "Getting a Review is Simple." As long as you're willing to pay $425 for Standard Delivery, or $575 for Express.

Will reviews help sell your book? Maybe not ones from your mother or Aunt Sally, but certainly a positive Kirkus Review will bring attention to your book. But are there other ways to gain public credibility and increase exposure? Yes. Contests.

Pick up any copy of *Writer's Digest*, *The Writer Magazine*, *Writers and Poets*, or any of the other dozens of genre-specific writing periodicals and in the back, you will find lists of contests. The entry fees can range from free (with a complimentary copy of the magazine as the prize) to hundreds of dollars, but one thing is for certain: if you win one of these contests, **it will help sell your books**. I am proof positive of that fact.

I entered my first, self-published title in the New York Book Festival in 2016, and ended up the Runner-Up in the Romance division. For my meager $50 entry fee, I was invited to the Awards Banquet (for an additional fee), given the podium to talk about my book for a whole three minutes, and received a nifty, framed certificate announcing my win. Does this sound hokey? Maybe it is. But you know what? I have (so far) sold over a hundred copies of that book simply because it was named a winner in the contest. And that book continues to be my bestseller because at the top of the description page it says, "Winner, 2016 NY Book Festival."

I highly recommend entering contests. Now, don't go crazy and spend thousands of dollars that you'll never recoup, and don't enter every contest that comes along. Be selective—you have the ability to choose your competition. For example, there are Book Festival competitions in most major cities—there's a Boston Book Festival, and I live in Massachusetts. So why did I enter the New York competition? Simple. First, the Boston contest did not have a specific category for Romance, which is the main genre of my book. Second, my book is set in New York. I knew I would stand a much, much better chance of a win, placement, or showing in the New York competition than in the Boston one, where my book would have been lumped in with the umpteen-thousand other "fiction" entries.

Set up a budget where contest entry fees are part of your advertising expenses. Decide how much per year you are willing to spend on contests, and enter accordingly. Don't expect to win every one. Don't expect to win any. But if you do, use that information as a giant, shining badge of honor. Add it to the top of your book description page and shout it out on every social media channel you utilize. *It will sell books*, I promise.

Now, will I enter this same book in another contest? No. I did enter it in a *cover* contest on Authorsdb—which it won—but that was free. But as far as I'm concerned, this book has proven its merit by winning in the NY Book Festival. I will now spend my contest fee dollars on my other books, until one of them, too, wins something. Once the book has a title win to its name, it has credibility. I won't waste any more money beating a . . .winning book. It simply doesn't make sense.

Closing Thoughts

I realize I've packed an awful lot of information into a hundred or so pages, but I hope I've provided a useful guide for those of you who are approaching this journey to publication. You now know how the publishing biz works, and hopefully have decided which route you want to pursue. As I said at the beginning, I wish I could have found a book like this when I first started out. I felt like the kid at the birthday party who had a bandanna tied around his head and got spun around three times before seeking to pin the tail on the donkey.

No, it was worse than that. It was like being thrust into a dark, tangled forest, crisscrossed with trails, with no earthly idea which one to take. I knew only one thing: what my pot of gold looked like. And I suggest that you, before you embark on any of these routes I've discussed, seriously consider what, *exactly what*, your publishing pot of gold looks like. Only then will you be able to decide which route is the right one for you.

Keep in mind that there are dozens, if not hundreds of other books out there on each and every particular aspect of this journey I have discussed. This was designed as an overview, a map, to give you an idea of the lay of the land. Now, study the map, and schedule your itinerary. One thing I know for certain—if you want that prize at the end of the journey—YOUR NOVEL—in whatever format you want, you can make it a reality.

And now for the four, most important words in this entire book:

JUST DON'T GIVE UP.

The Road to Publication

A Note from the Author

Thank you for joining me on this lively jaunt through the world of Publication. I hope the information I've provided is useful to you in your quest, and that I've kept you somewhat entertained.

If you'd like to check out some of my fiction books I've mentioned throughout, you can find them at my Amazon Author Page. I also invite you to check out my website and blog, where you can sign up for my newsletters. You will be given a choice of which newsletter you want to join: fiction or nonfiction. Then you'll be the first to know when the next of my Author Resource books becomes available without cluttering your inbox with books about love stories or scary ghosts.

You can also connect with me on Facebook, Twitter, and Goodreads. I love hearing from readers—feel free to drop me a line anytime with feedback (good or bad!), as well as with suggestions as to what information you'd like to see in my next Author Resource series book.

Remember: Once you've published that first book, the very best thing you can do to sell more books is to write the next one. So, fire up your keyboard and get writing!

Website: http://www.clairegem.com
Blog: http://www.clairegem.wordpress.com
Facebook: http://www.facebook.com/clairegem.author
Twitter: http://www.twitter.com/gemwriter
Goodreads: http://bit.ly/17zCJwY

REFERENCES

Here is a list of the websites I have referred to throughout the book, in alphabetical order.

Amazon Kindle Categories: http://amzn.to/2mj1SF3
Authorsdb: http://www.authorsdb.com
Authorhouse: http://www.authorhouse.com
Bookow: http://www.bookow.com
Bowker Identifier Services:
https://www.myidentifiers.com
Calibre: http://www.calibre.com
Carbonite: http://www.carbonite.com
Createspace: http://www.createspace.com
Depositphotos: http://www.depositphotos.com
Draft2Digital: http://www.draft2digital.com
GoDaddy: http://www.godaddy.com
Instafreebie: http://www.instafreebie.com
Kirkus Reviews: http://www.kirkusreviews.com
List of 100 Least Competitive Amazon Kindle Categories:
http://bit.ly/2mYgQ6l
Pixabay: http://www.pixabay.com
Scrivener: http://www.literatureandlatte.com
Silver Sparrow Editorial:
http://www.silversparroweditorial.com
The New York Times: https://www.nytimes.coM

The Writer's Market: http://www.writersmarket.com

Vistaprint: http://www.vistaprint.com
Writer's Toolbox: http://bit.ly/2mlMb1c

www.ingramcontent.com/pod-product-compliance
Lightning Source LLC
Chambersburg PA
CBHW071311060426
42444CB00034B/1769